THE ART OF MUSCLE BUILDING

Techniques and Tactics for Success

SREEKUMAR V T

PREFACE

Welcome to "The Art of Muscle Building: Techniques and Tactics for Success." This book is a comprehensive guide that explores the science, strategies, and mindset required to master the craft of sculpting a powerful, well-developed physique. Whether you are a seasoned gym enthusiast, a beginner taking your first steps into the world of strength training, or someone simply seeking to improve their fitness, this book is designed to be your trusted companion on your journey to muscle development success.

The pursuit of muscle building is not just a physical endeavour; it is an art form. It involves the precise application of techniques, strategies, and principles to create a work of art that is your body. It's a journey that demands dedication, perseverance, and a deep understanding of the intricate interplay between nutrition, training, and recovery.

Within these pages, you will find a wealth of knowledge, from the fundamentals of muscle growth to advanced strategies that will help you optimize your results. We delve into the art of setting clear and achievable goals, constructing effective workout programs, and harnessing the power of nutrition to fuel your progress. You'll explore the principles of progressive overload, learn how to maximize muscle hypertrophy, and master the essentials of strength training. We also cover the role of cardio and conditioning, the importance of recovery and rest, and the potential benefits and limitations of various supplements.

To help you navigate the potential pitfalls along the way, we provide guidance on injury prevention and management, as well as tools to track and measure your progress accurately. The mental aspect of muscle building is not overlooked, as we delve into motivation and the mental toughness required to stay committed to your goals.

Throughout the book, you'll discover practical advice, real-life success stories, and case studies that illustrate the principles and techniques discussed. We've aimed to create a resource that is accessible and actionable, ensuring that you can apply what you learn directly to your own fitness journey.

Whether your goal is to build strength, gain muscle, or simply improve your overall health and well-being, "The Art of Muscle Building" is your guide to success. We hope this book serves as a source of inspiration, knowledge, and motivation as you embark on your own unique path to a stronger, more muscular you.

The art of muscle building is a journey that can be both challenging and rewarding, and we are excited to be your companions on this path. So, let's get started on the road to building the body you've always envisioned, one chapter at a time. Your masterpiece awaits!

COPYRIGHT WARNING NOTICE

All rights reserved. No part of this publication may be reproduced, distributed, or transmitted in any form or by any means, including photocopying, recording, or other electronic or mechanical methods, without the prior written permission of the copyright holder, except in the case of brief quotations embodied in critical reviews and certain other non-commercial uses permitted by copyright law.

Unauthorized reproduction or distribution of this copyrighted work is illegal and may be subject to civil and criminal penalties. Any use of the content, including but not limited to copying, adapting, or sharing, without the express written permission of the copyright holder is strictly prohibited and will be pursued to the full extent of the law.

© 2023 by [Your Name or Publishing Company]

For permissions and inquiries regarding the use of content from this book, please contact:

Vtsreekumar123@gmail.com

Every effort has been made to ensure that the information in this book is accurate; however, the author and the publisher do not assume and hereby disclaim any liability to any party for any loss, damage, or disruption caused by errors or omissions, whether such errors or omissions result from negligence, accident, or any other cause.

CONTENTS

1. The Fundamentals of Muscle Building
2. Setting Clear Goals and Objectives
3. Nutrition for Muscle Growth
4. Effective Workout Programming
5. Progressive Overload Techniques
6. Maximizing Muscle Hypertrophy
7. Strength Training Principles
8. Cardio and Conditioning for Muscle Builders
9. Recovery and Rest Days
10. Supplements for Muscle Enhancement
11. Injury Prevention and Management
12. Tracking and Measuring Progress
13. Motivation and Mental Toughness
14. Fine-Tuning Your Routine for Results
15. Case Studies and Success Stories

1. THE FUNDAMENTALS OF MUSCLE BUILDING

Muscle building is an intricate and fascinating process that, when understood and executed correctly, can lead to incredible transformations in the human body. Whether you're a seasoned bodybuilder or just starting on your fitness journey, grasping the fundamentals of muscle building is crucial to achieving the results you desire. In this chapter, we will explore the science behind muscle growth, the key principles that govern the process, and how to apply these fundamentals to sculpt the physique of your dreams.

The Science of Muscle Growth

Before diving into the practical aspects of muscle building, it's essential to understand the underlying science. Muscles are made up of thousands of individual muscle fibers, and muscle growth, or hypertrophy, occurs when these fibers increase in size and number.

Types of Muscle Fibers

There are two primary types of muscle fibers in the human body: slow-twitch (Type I) and fast-twitch (Type II) fibers. Slow-twitch fibers are more endurance-oriented and are responsible for activities such as long-distance running. Fast-twitch fibers, on the other hand, are more suited for explosive, high-intensity activities like weightlifting and sprinting.

The Role of Resistance Training

Resistance training, which includes weightlifting and bodyweight exercises, plays a central role in muscle building. When you engage in resistance training, your muscle fibers are subjected to mechanical stress. This stress, in the form of resistance or weight, creates tiny micro-tears in the muscle fibers. As a response to these micro-tears, the body initiates a repair and growth process.

Protein Synthesis

Central to muscle growth is a phenomenon known as protein synthesis. After resistance training, the body increases protein synthesis, which is the process of building new proteins. This is when muscle fibers repair and become thicker and stronger.

The Key Principles of Muscle Building

Now that we've established the scientific foundation of muscle growth, let's delve into the key principles that underpin this process. Understanding these principles is crucial for designing effective workout programs and achieving optimal results.

Progressive Overload

Progressive overload is arguably the most critical principle of muscle building. It involves gradually increasing the resistance or weight you lift over time. By consistently challenging your muscles with heavier loads, you stimulate continuous growth. Without progressive overload, your muscles will have no reason to adapt and become stronger.

To implement progressive overload, you can increase the weight you lift, perform more repetitions with the same weight, or reduce the rest periods between sets. A well-structured workout program will incorporate progressive overload to ensure steady muscle growth.

Volume and Intensity

Volume and intensity are two key variables in muscle building. Volume refers to the total amount of work performed in a workout, typically measured by the number of sets and repetitions. Intensity, on the other hand, relates to how close you are to your one-repetition maximum (1RM) – the maximum weight you can lift for a single repetition.

To promote muscle growth, you'll need to find the right balance between volume and intensity. Higher volume (more sets and repetitions) with moderate intensity can induce hypertrophy, while lower volume with higher intensity is more focused on strength gains.

Muscle Time Under Tension (TUT)

Muscle time under tension (TUT) is the duration that a muscle is actively engaged during a set. The longer a muscle is under tension, the more it's stressed, and the greater the potential for hypertrophy. This is why controlling the tempo of your repetitions can be beneficial. For instance, performing slower eccentric (lengthening) and concentric (shortening) phases of a repetition can increase TUT.

Exercise Selection

Not all exercises are created equal when it comes to muscle building. Compound exercises, which involve multiple muscle groups, are particularly effective for overall muscle growth. Exercises like squats, deadlifts, bench presses, and pull-ups engage a wide range of muscle fibers, leading to significant gains.

Isolation exercises, which target specific muscle groups, can be valuable for targeting lagging areas or achieving aesthetic goals. However, they should be used in conjunction with compound exercises for a well-rounded approach.

Rest and Recovery

Muscle growth doesn't happen during your workouts; it occurs during the recovery phase. Rest and recovery are essential for allowing your muscles to repair and adapt to the stress placed on them during training. Overtraining, which occurs when you don't allow sufficient recovery time, can hinder progress and increase the risk of injury.

Adequate sleep, proper nutrition, and smart training programming are key components of recovery. Sleep is particularly crucial as it is when the body releases growth hormone and facilitates muscle repair.

Designing an Effective Workout Program

Understanding the principles of muscle building is only half the battle. To put this knowledge into practice, you need to design a well-structured workout program that incorporates these fundamentals. Here's a step-by-step guide to creating an effective muscle-building program:

Step 1: Set Clear Goals

Begin by defining your muscle-building goals. Do you want to gain overall muscle mass, focus on strength, or target specific muscle groups? Having clear objectives will guide your program design.

Step 2: Choose the Right Exercises

Select a combination of compound and isolation exercises that align with your goals. Compound exercises should form the core of your program, while isolation exercises can be included as needed.

Step 3: Determine Your Training Split

A training split defines how you organize your workouts throughout the week. Common splits include full-body workouts, upper/lower body splits, and muscle group-specific splits. The choice should align with your goals and schedule.

Step 4: Establish Repetition Ranges

Based on your goals, determine the number of repetitions you'll perform for each exercise. For muscle building, a range of 6-12 repetitions per set is typically effective. Adjust this range according to your goals, with lower repetitions for strength and higher repetitions for endurance.

Step 5: Plan Your Progression

Incorporate progressive overload into your program by gradually increasing the resistance or weight you lift. Keep track of your workouts to ensure you're consistently challenging yourself.

Step 6: Consider Rest and Recovery

Determine the rest intervals between sets and exercises. Generally, 2-3 minutes of rest is suitable for muscle building, allowing sufficient recovery without excessive downtime.

Step 7: Incorporate Variation

Periodically change your exercises, set and repetition schemes, and workout structure to prevent plateaus and keep your workouts engaging.

Step 8: Focus on Nutrition

Nutrition is a crucial aspect of muscle building. Ensure you're consuming an adequate amount of calories, protein, carbohydrates, and healthy fats to support muscle growth and recovery.

Step 9: Monitor Your Progress

Regularly track your progress by recording your workouts, taking measurements, and assessing your strength gains. Adjust your program as needed to continue making progress.

Nutrition for Muscle Building

Nutrition is the fuel that powers your muscle-building journey. Without the right balance of nutrients, your body won't have the necessary building blocks to repair and grow muscle tissue. Here are some fundamental principles of nutrition for muscle building:

Caloric Surplus

To gain muscle mass, you need to consume more calories than your body burns. This creates a caloric surplus that provides the energy needed for muscle growth. Aim for a moderate surplus, as excessive caloric intake can lead to excessive fat gain.

Protein Intake

Protein is essential for muscle repair and growth. A sufficient protein intake ensures that your body has the amino acids required for building and repairing muscle fibers. Aim for around 1.2 to 2.2 grams of protein per kilogram of body weight per day.

Carbohydrates and Fats

Carbohydrates are the body's primary energy source, and fats play a crucial role in hormone production. Both should be part of a balanced diet. Carbohydrates fuel your workouts, and fats are essential for overall health.

Hydration

Proper hydration is often overlooked but is vital for muscle function and overall health. Dehydration can lead to decreased exercise performance and hinder muscle recovery.

Meal Timing

Spacing your meals throughout the day ensures a consistent intake of nutrients and energy. Pre- and post-workout meals are particularly important to provide your body with the necessary fuel and nutrients.

Supplements

While supplements should never replace a balanced diet, they can be used to complement your nutrition. Common muscle-building supplements include protein powders, creatine, and branched-chain amino acids (BCAAs).

Conclusion

Understanding the fundamentals of muscle building is the foundation upon which you can build a successful and effective workout program. With knowledge of the science of muscle growth, key principles such as progressive overload, and the critical role of nutrition, you have the tools to embark on a journey of transformation.

Remember that consistency, dedication, and patience are key to achieving your muscle-building goals. Muscle growth takes time, and there are no shortcuts. By applying the principles outlined in this chapter and tailoring them to your unique needs and aspirations, you can create a roadmap to the physique you've always dreamed of.

In the upcoming chapters of "The Art of Muscle Building: Techniques and Tactics for Success," we will explore more advanced strategies, exercise routines, and nutritional guidance to help you maximize your muscle-building potential. So, continue your journey with us, and let's sculpt the masterpiece that is your body, one rep at a time.

2. SETTING CLEAR GOALS AND OBJECTIVES

In the pursuit of building a strong, well-defined physique, setting clear goals and objectives is not just a suggestion; it's an absolute necessity. Without a roadmap to guide your muscle-building journey, you risk wandering aimlessly and never achieving the results you desire. In this chapter, we will explore the importance of goal setting in the context of muscle building, how to establish clear and realistic objectives, and the role that goal setting plays in maintaining motivation and tracking progress.
The Power of Clear Goals

Imagine embarking on a cross-country road trip without a destination in mind. You start driving, but with no clear endpoint, you're left meandering from one direction to another, making random turns at intersections, and never truly making progress. This lack of direction can lead to frustration, confusion, and ultimately, the abandonment of your journey.

The same principle applies to muscle building. Without defined goals, you risk wandering aimlessly through your workouts, making inconsistent decisions about your nutrition, and not fully realizing your potential. Your journey becomes a never-ending cycle of trial and error, where you're never entirely sure if you're on the right path or if you've made any progress at all.

The Benefits of Goal Setting

Setting clear, well-defined goals in your muscle-building journey offers a multitude of advantages:

1. **Direction:** Goals provide a clear direction, allowing you to focus your efforts on a specific outcome.
2. **Motivation:** Having something to strive for keeps you motivated and committed to your training and nutrition plan.
3. **Measurability:** Goals make it possible to track your progress and assess whether you're moving in the right direction.
4. **Accountability:** Clear objectives hold you accountable to yourself. You're more likely to stick to your plan when you have a specific target in mind.
5. **Efficiency:** When you have a purpose, you can structure your workouts and nutrition to achieve your objectives more efficiently.
6. **Satisfaction:** Achieving your goals is rewarding and boosts your confidence, making it easier to stay committed to the process.

Types of Muscle-Building Goals

When setting goals for muscle building, it's important to categorize them into different types. Here are the three primary types of goals to consider:

Short-Term Goals

Short-term goals are those you aim to achieve within a relatively short timeframe, typically ranging from a few weeks to a few months. These goals serve as stepping stones towards your larger, long-term objectives. Short-term goals can be specific, such as increasing the weight you lift in a particular exercise or reducing your body fat percentage.

Long-Term Goals

Long-term goals are the bigger picture. These are the objectives you hope to achieve over an extended period, often spanning several months or even years. They could include gaining a certain amount of muscle mass, reaching a specific body fat percentage, or competing in a bodybuilding competition. Long-term goals require dedication and consistent effort.

Performance Goals

Performance goals focus on improving your physical abilities, such as increasing your strength, endurance, or flexibility. These goals can be tied to specific exercises or movements. For example, you might aim to squat a certain amount of weight or complete a marathon within a certain time frame.

When setting muscle-building goals, consider incorporating a mix of short-term and long-term objectives, along with performance goals that keep your workouts challenging and engaging.

SMART Goal Setting

An effective way to set clear and actionable goals is by using the SMART criteria. SMART stands for Specific, Measurable, Achievable, Relevant, and Time-bound. Let's break down each component:

Specific

Your goals should be clearly defined and leave no room for ambiguity. Instead of a vague goal like "I want to get in better shape," aim for something specific, such as "I want to increase my lean muscle mass by 10%."

Measurable

Your goals should be quantifiable. You should be able to track and measure your progress objectively. For instance, "I want to bench press 200 pounds" is measurable, while "I want to get stronger" is not.

Achievable

Your goals should be realistic and attainable. While it's great to dream big, setting unattainable goals can lead to discouragement. Assess your current capabilities and progress incrementally from there. For example, if you can currently bench press 150 pounds, aiming for 200 pounds is achievable.

Relevant

Your goals should be aligned with your personal values and priorities. They should have meaning and relevance to your life. Goals that resonate with you are more likely to keep you motivated.

Time-bound

Your goals should have a specific timeframe for completion. This adds a sense of urgency and prevents procrastination. Instead of saying, "I want to gain muscle," say, "I want to gain 10 pounds of muscle in the next six months."

Crafting Your Muscle-Building Objectives

Now that you understand the importance of setting clear goals and the SMART criteria, it's time to craft your muscle-building objectives. Here's a step-by-step process to guide you:

Step 1: Define Your Long-Term Goals

Begin by identifying your ultimate long-term objectives. What do you want to achieve in the world of muscle building? This could be a target body weight, a certain body fat percentage, or the ability to perform specific exercises with a certain amount of weight.

Step 2: Break Down Your Long-Term Goals

Once you have your long-term goals in mind, break them down into smaller, manageable short-term objectives. These will serve as milestones along your journey.

Step 3: Apply the SMART Criteria

Refine your goals using the SMART criteria. Ensure they are specific, measurable, achievable, relevant, and time-bound.

Step 4: Write Your Goals Down

Don't keep your goals in your head. Write them down on paper or in a digital document. This step makes your objectives tangible and reinforces your commitment to them.

Step 5: Create an Action Plan

With your goals in place, create an action plan outlining the steps you need to take to achieve them. Consider factors like your workout routine, nutrition, and any additional strategies required.

Step 6: Set Performance Goals

Incorporate performance goals into your plan. These could include increasing the weight you lift, improving your flexibility, or achieving specific fitness milestones.

The Role of Goal Setting in Motivation

Goal setting is closely intertwined with motivation. When you have clear objectives, you are more likely to stay motivated and dedicated to your fitness journey. Here's how goal setting boosts motivation:

1. Provides a Purpose

Goals give you a reason to wake up early for that morning workout or resist the temptation of unhealthy food. They provide a clear purpose for your actions.

2. Maintains Focus

When you have well-defined goals, you stay focused on what you want to achieve. This concentration helps you push through challenges and setbacks.

3. Measures Progress

Goals act as yardsticks to measure your progress. Tracking your achievements, no matter how small, is highly motivating and reinforces your commitment to your journey.

4. Celebrates Success

Reaching a goal is a cause for celebration. Recognizing your achievements, no matter how minor, provides a sense of accomplishment that fuels your motivation to set and achieve more goals.

5. Overcomes Plateaus

Inevitably, you will face plateaus and periods of slow progress in your muscle-building journey. Having goals in place helps you break through these plateaus by adjusting your approach and pushing past limitations.

Tracking Progress and Adjusting Goals

Goal setting is not a one-time event; it's an ongoing process. Regularly tracking your progress and evaluating your goals are essential for staying on track and adapting to changes. Here's how to effectively track your progress and adjust your goals:

1. Record Workouts

Keep a detailed workout journal to track your exercises, sets, repetitions, and the amount of weight lifted. This data will help you identify patterns and make necessary adjustments to your training plan.

2. Regular Assessments

Schedule regular assessments of your progress. This could include body measurements, body fat percentage assessments, and strength testing. Use these assessments to evaluate whether you're moving closer to your goals.

3. Adjust as Needed

Don't be afraid to modify your goals or your approach if you're not making the progress you desire. Sometimes, factors such as lifestyle changes, injuries, or new priorities may necessitate goal adjustments.

4. Seek Professional Guidance

Consider consulting with a fitness professional or a coach to help you set and adjust your goals. They can provide expert advice and support to ensure your goals are both challenging and attainable.

Goal Setting and Mental Toughness

The process of setting and pursuing muscle-building goals is not only a physical endeavor but also a mental one. It requires mental toughness to stay committed, push through challenges, and persist when results aren't immediate. Here's how goal setting contributes to mental strength:

1. Discipline

Setting and pursuing goals instills discipline in your training and nutrition habits. Discipline is the key to maintaining consistency and resilience in the face of obstacles.

2. Resilience

Muscle building is a journey filled with ups and downs. Goals help you develop resilience by encouraging you to persevere through difficulties, learn from setbacks, and bounce back stronger.

3. Focus

Clear goals keep you focused on your objectives, preventing distractions and deviations from your path. This unwavering focus is a hallmark of mental toughness.

4. Self-Belief

Achieving goals boosts your self-belief and confidence. This self-assurance strengthens your mental fortitude and encourages you to set even more ambitious objectives.

Conclusion

Setting clear goals and objectives is the cornerstone of successful muscle building. Your goals give you a sense of purpose, motivate you, and provide a roadmap to guide your journey. The SMART criteria enable you to refine your objectives, making them specific, measurable, achievable, relevant, and time-bound.

As you progress on your muscle-building journey, regularly track your achievements and be prepared to adjust your goals as needed. Remember that goal setting is not just about physical transformation; it's also a mental endeavor that cultivates discipline, resilience, and self-belief.

In the chapters to come, we will delve deeper into the strategies and tactics that will help you achieve your muscle-building goals. From workout programming to nutrition planning and recovery techniques, you'll find a comprehensive guide to sculpting the body of your dreams. So, set your goals, stay committed, and embrace the process as you embark on your transformation in "The Art of Muscle Building: Techniques and Tactics for Success." Your journey has just begun, and your potential is limitless.

3. NUTRITION FOR MUSCLE GROWTH

Nutrition is the unsung hero of muscle building. While the gym might be where you break down muscle fibers and create the stimulus for growth, it's in the kitchen where you provide your body with the essential building blocks and energy needed for that growth. In this chapter, we'll explore the critical role that nutrition plays in muscle development, offering insights into macronutrients, meal timing, supplements, and dietary strategies to maximize your muscle-building potential.

The Nutritional Foundation of Muscle Growth

To understand how nutrition fuels muscle growth, we need to break it down into its core components: macronutrients and micronutrients.

Macronutrients

Macronutrients are the primary nutrients your body needs in large quantities to function properly. In the context of muscle building, there are three key macronutrients:

1. Protein

Protein is the holy grail of muscle building. It's the primary building block of muscle tissue, consisting of amino acids, and plays a crucial role in muscle repair and growth. Consuming an adequate amount of high-quality protein in your diet is essential to support muscle development.

2. Carbohydrates

Carbohydrates are the body's primary energy source. When you engage in resistance training and other physical activities, your body relies on carbohydrates to provide the energy needed for your workouts. Carbohydrates also replenish glycogen stores in your muscles, which are essential for endurance and high-intensity activities.

3. Fats

Fats are often overlooked in muscle building, but they are vital for overall health and hormonal balance. Essential fatty acids support hormone production, which influences muscle growth. Additionally, fats help absorb fat-soluble vitamins that contribute to various metabolic processes in the body.

Micronutrients

Micronutrients, which include vitamins and minerals, are essential for various bodily functions. They support overall health and are indirectly involved in muscle building by maintaining the proper functioning of systems like the immune and endocrine systems. Ensuring you have a balanced intake of vitamins and minerals through a diverse diet is crucial for muscle growth and overall well-being.

Protein: The Muscle Builder's Best Friend

As previously mentioned, protein is the cornerstone of muscle building. It provides the amino acids necessary to repair and grow muscle tissue. Let's delve deeper into the role of protein in muscle development:

Amino Acids

Amino acids are the individual building blocks of proteins, and they come in two categories: essential and non-essential. Essential amino acids cannot be produced by the body and must be obtained through your diet. They are crucial for muscle protein synthesis, the process by which your body repairs and builds muscle tissue.

Leucine

Leucine, an essential amino acid, plays a particularly pivotal role in muscle protein synthesis. It acts as a signal to initiate the process, making it a critical component of any muscle-building diet. Foods rich in leucine include lean meats, dairy products, and certain plant-based sources like legumes.

Protein Timing

The timing of your protein intake can influence muscle growth. Consuming protein both before and after your workout is beneficial for muscle protein synthesis. Pre-workout protein provides amino acids for your muscles to use during exercise, while post-workout protein supports recovery and growth. Aim to consume protein-rich meals or snacks within an hour or two of your workout.

Protein Sources

High-quality protein sources are essential for muscle building. Consider including the following in your diet:

- Lean meats: Chicken, turkey, lean cuts of beef, and pork.
- Fish: Salmon, tuna, and other fatty fish.
- Eggs: A complete source of protein.
- Dairy: Greek yogurt, cottage cheese, and milk.
- Plant-based sources: Legumes, tofu, tempeh, and seitan.
- Protein supplements: Whey, casein, or plant-based protein powders.

Carbohydrates: Fueling Your Workouts

Carbohydrates are the primary energy source your body relies on during resistance training and other physical activities. Here's how they play a crucial role in muscle growth:

Energy for Workouts

Carbohydrates provide the quick and accessible energy your muscles need for resistance training. Complex carbohydrates, such as whole grains, vegetables, and legumes, are excellent sources of sustained energy for your workouts.

Glycogen Replenishment

Glycogen is a form of stored glucose in your muscles and liver. During intense exercise, your body depletes its glycogen stores. Consuming carbohydrates after your workout helps replenish these stores, ensuring you have adequate energy for your next training session.

Carbohydrate Timing

While it's important to consume carbohydrates throughout the day, emphasizing carbohydrate intake around your workouts can be particularly beneficial. A carbohydrate-rich meal or snack 1-2 hours before exercise can help ensure you have the energy to train effectively.

Fats: The Unsung Heroes

Fats play an essential role in muscle building and overall health. They are not to be feared but embraced in your nutrition plan:

Hormone Production

Fats, especially healthy fats like those found in avocados, nuts, and fatty fish, are essential for hormone production. Hormones like testosterone and growth hormone are key players in muscle development.

Nutrient Absorption

Many vitamins, such as vitamins A, D, E, and K, are fat-soluble, meaning they require dietary fats for proper absorption. These vitamins are essential for various metabolic processes that indirectly support muscle growth.

Caloric Surplus

Fats are calorie-dense, which can be advantageous if you need to maintain a caloric surplus to support muscle growth. Including sources of healthy fats in your diet can help you meet your energy requirements.

Meal Timing and Frequency

The timing and frequency of your meals and snacks can impact muscle growth. Consider these strategies for optimizing your meal schedule:

Pre-Workout Nutrition

A well-balanced meal or snack containing a combination of carbohydrates, protein, and healthy fats 1-2 hours before your workout can provide your body with the necessary nutrients and energy to excel during your training session.

Post-Workout Nutrition

After your workout, aim to consume a meal or snack rich in protein and carbohydrates within an hour or two. This timing is crucial for replenishing glycogen stores and initiating muscle recovery and growth.

Meal Frequency

The number of meals you consume daily can vary based on personal preference and lifestyle. Some individuals prefer three larger meals, while others thrive on six smaller, evenly spaced meals. Find the meal frequency that suits your schedule and helps you meet your nutritional goals.

Nutrient Timing

Strategically timing your nutrient intake around your workouts is beneficial. However, it's important to note that overall daily nutrient intake remains the most crucial factor. As long as you meet your daily nutritional needs, the timing of individual meals and snacks becomes a matter of personal preference and convenience.

Supplements for Muscle Growth

While the foundation of your nutrition should be a well-balanced whole-food diet, supplements can be valuable in ensuring you meet your specific nutritional requirements. Here are some supplements to consider for muscle building:

Protein Supplements

Protein supplements, such as whey and casein protein powders, are convenient sources of high-quality protein. They can be especially useful if you struggle to meet your protein needs through whole foods alone.

Creatine

Creatine is one of the most researched and effective supplements for increasing strength and muscle mass. It helps provide energy during high-intensity, short-duration activities like weightlifting.

Branched-Chain Amino Acids (BCAAs)

BCAAs, which include leucine, isoleucine, and valine, can support muscle protein synthesis, reduce muscle soreness, and enhance recovery. They are often used as a supplement to aid muscle building and exercise performance.

Beta-Alanine

Beta-alanine can help increase endurance and reduce muscle fatigue, allowing you to push harder during your workouts.

Multivitamins and Minerals

While supplements are not a substitute for a balanced diet, a high-quality multivitamin and mineral supplement can help ensure you're meeting your daily micronutrient needs.

Dietary Strategies for Muscle Building

In addition to understanding macronutrients, meal timing, and supplements, there are specific dietary strategies you can employ to optimize muscle growth:

Caloric Surplus

To gain muscle mass, you need to be in a caloric surplus, which means you're consuming more calories than your body burns. This surplus provides the energy required for muscle growth. While the exact surplus needed varies from person to person, aim for a modest surplus to minimize fat gain.

Balanced Nutrition

A well-rounded diet that includes a mix of protein, carbohydrates, and healthy fats is crucial. Don't focus solely on one macronutrient at the expense of others. Balance is key for overall health and muscle development.

Hydration

Proper hydration is often underestimated but is vital for muscle function and overall health. Dehydration can lead to decreased exercise performance and hinder muscle recovery.

Fiber Intake

Fiber is important for digestion and overall health. Include fiber-rich foods like vegetables, fruits, whole grains, and legumes in your diet to support digestive health.

Variety

A diverse diet not only provides a broad spectrum of nutrients but also makes eating enjoyable. Experiment with different foods, flavors, and cuisines to keep your diet interesting and sustainable.

Tracking Your Nutrition

Consistency in your nutrition is essential for muscle growth. One effective way to ensure you're meeting your nutritional goals is by tracking your food intake. Here are a few methods you can use:

Food Journal

Keep a food journal where you record everything you eat and drink. This can be done with a physical notebook or a smartphone app. Monitoring your meals and snacks helps you identify trends and adjust your diet accordingly.

Meal Prep

Planning and preparing your meals in advance can help you control your portions and make healthier choices. Meal prep also saves time and ensures you have access to nutritious food when you need it.

Calorie and Macronutrient Tracking

If you have specific calorie and macronutrient targets, you can use nutrition tracking apps or online tools to monitor your intake. These tools make it easy to see if you're hitting your nutritional goals.

Conclusion

Nutrition is the unsung hero of muscle building, providing the essential building blocks and energy for growth. By understanding the role of macronutrients, meal timing, and supplements, and employing dietary strategies, you can optimize your nutrition for muscle development.

Remember that nutrition is not a one-size-fits-all approach. Tailor your diet to your specific needs, preferences, and goals. Consistency, balance, and adequate energy intake are key to achieving muscle-building success.

In the following chapters of "The Art of Muscle Building: Techniques and Tactics for Success," we will delve deeper into workout programming, recovery strategies, and additional tips to maximize your muscle-building potential. As you continue your journey, you'll discover the art and science of transforming your body into a powerful, well-defined masterpiece. Your potential is boundless, and your path to success begins with the fuel you provide your body.

4. EFFECTIVE WORKOUT PROGRAMMING

Effective workout programming is the cornerstone of achieving your muscle-building goals. It's not just about lifting weights; it's about following a structured plan that strategically targets different muscle groups, optimizes progressive overload, and promotes growth while minimizing the risk of injury. In this chapter, we will explore the key principles and strategies of effective workout programming, including split routines, exercise selection, rep and set schemes, and periodization.

The Art of Workout Programming

Creating an effective workout program is akin to composing a symphony. Each exercise, set, and repetition should be harmoniously orchestrated to produce the desired result – muscle growth. Let's delve into the fundamental principles of workout programming and how they work together to create a masterpiece of muscle development.

Progressive Overload

The bedrock of effective workout programming is the principle of progressive overload. It's the art of gradually increasing the resistance or weight you lift over time. Progressive overload ensures that your muscles are consistently challenged, leading to adaptation and growth.

Without progressive overload, your muscles have no reason to get bigger and stronger. It's crucial to structure your program to systematically increase the intensity of your workouts. Here are several ways to incorporate progressive overload into your training plan:

- **Increase Weight:** Gradually add more weight to your exercises as you become stronger. For example, if you're bench pressing 100 pounds, aim to lift 105 pounds in your next session.
- **Add Repetitions:** Perform more repetitions with the same weight. If you can do 3 sets of 8 reps with a 20-pound dumbbell, work towards 3 sets of 10 reps with the same weight.
- **Reduce Rest Periods:** Shorten the rest intervals between sets and exercises. This can make your workouts more challenging and encourage adaptation.
- **Adjust Tempo:** Manipulate the tempo of your repetitions. Slower eccentric (lengthening) and concentric (shortening) phases of a repetition can increase the time under tension and promote growth.

Exercise Selection

Selecting the right exercises is another crucial aspect of effective workout programming. The goal is to choose exercises that target the specific muscle groups you want to develop. Exercises can be broadly categorized into two types:

Compound Exercises

Compound exercises involve multiple muscle groups and joints. They are excellent for overall muscle development, as they engage a wide range of muscle fibers. Common compound exercises include squats, deadlifts, bench presses, pull-ups, and rows.

Isolation Exercises

Isolation exercises focus on specific muscle groups. They are valuable for targeting weaker or lagging areas and achieving aesthetic goals. Examples of isolation exercises include bicep curls, leg extensions, and tricep pushdowns.

Your workout program should strike a balance between compound and isolation exercises. Compound movements should form the core of your routine, targeting large muscle groups, while isolation exercises can be used strategically to address specific areas of interest or weaknesses.

Repetition and Set Schemes

The way you structure your repetitions and sets plays a significant role in achieving your muscle-building goals. Different repetition and set schemes produce varying results. Here are some common schemes and their effects:

High Repetition, Low Weight

High-repetition, low-weight schemes (e.g., 3 sets of 15-20 reps) are often used for muscle endurance and hypertrophy. This approach increases the time under tension, promoting muscle growth, and improving muscular endurance.

Moderate Repetition, Moderate Weight

Moderate repetition, moderate-weight schemes (e.g., 3 sets of 8-12 reps) are a popular choice for overall muscle development. They balance strength and hypertrophy and are suitable for most individuals.

Low Repetition, High Weight

Low-repetition, high-weight schemes (e.g., 4 sets of 4-6 reps) focus on developing strength and power. While these schemes might not induce maximal hypertrophy, they are essential for building a strong foundation.

Pyramid Sets

Pyramid sets involve progressively increasing or decreasing the weight and repetitions in subsequent sets. This can be an effective way to challenge your muscles and stimulate growth.

The choice of repetition and set schemes depends on your individual goals. If you're primarily interested in muscle hypertrophy, moderate repetition schemes with adequate weight are a solid choice. However, it's also beneficial to incorporate variation into your routine to challenge your muscles and avoid plateaus.

Split Routines

Split routines are a crucial aspect of effective workout programming, especially for those with specific muscle-building goals. Instead of working your entire body in every workout, split routines divide your training into different muscle groups on different days. Common split routines include:

Upper/Lower Body Split

This split alternates between upper body and lower body workouts. It allows you to focus on specific muscle groups in each session while providing ample recovery time.

Push/Pull Split

The push/pull split divides exercises into pushing (e.g., chest, shoulders, triceps) and pulling (e.g., back, biceps) movements. This approach helps maintain balance in muscle development and can reduce the risk of overuse injuries.

Muscle Group Split

A muscle group split dedicates specific days to training particular muscle groups. For example, you might have a leg day, chest and triceps day, back and biceps day, and a shoulder day.

Full-Body Workouts

Full-body workouts engage all major muscle groups in a single session. They are effective for individuals with limited time and are excellent for overall muscle development.

The choice of split routine depends on your goals, preferences, and available time. Split routines allow you to focus on specific muscle groups more intensely and provide more time for recovery, which is crucial for muscle growth.

Periodization

Periodization is a systematic approach to structuring your workout program. It involves dividing your training into specific cycles, each with its own goals and focus. Periodization helps prevent plateaus, minimizes overuse injuries, and ensures continued progress. Here are the three primary phases of periodization:

1. **Anatomical Adaptation Phase**

During this phase, the emphasis is on building a solid foundation by targeting structural balance and muscular endurance. It typically involves higher repetition schemes and a variety of exercises to ensure balanced development.

2. Hypertrophy Phase

In the hypertrophy phase, the goal is to stimulate muscle growth. Repetition and set schemes typically fall into the moderate-repetition, moderate-weight range. Volume is increased, and compound and isolation exercises are used to target specific muscle groups.

3. Strength and Power Phase

The strength and power phase focuses on maximizing strength and power gains. Low-repetition, high-weight schemes are commonly employed. Compound exercises take center stage to develop raw strength.

Sample Periodization Plan

Here's a simplified example of how periodization can be incorporated into a workout program:

- **Weeks 1-4 (Anatomical Adaptation):** Emphasize balance and muscular endurance with higher repetition schemes. Incorporate a variety of exercises targeting different muscle groups.
- **Weeks 5-8 (Hypertrophy):** Transition to moderate-repetition, moderate-weight schemes to stimulate muscle growth. Focus on compound and isolation exercises for specific muscle groups.
- **Weeks 9-12 (Strength and Power):** Shift to low-repetition, high-weight schemes to maximize strength and power gains. Prioritize compound exercises for overall strength.

Periodization can be adapted and personalized based on your experience level, goals, and the time you have available for training.

Recovery and Rest

Effective workout programming also includes prioritizing recovery and rest. Adequate rest between workouts and individual sets is essential for muscle growth and injury prevention. Here are some key points to consider:

- **Rest Days:** Incorporate rest days into your program to allow your muscles to recover fully. Rest days are just as important as workout days.
- **Sleep:** Ensure you get sufficient quality sleep, as this is when your body primarily repairs and grows muscle tissue.
- **Nutrition:** Support your recovery with proper nutrition, including a post-workout meal rich in protein and carbohydrates.
- **Hydration:** Stay hydrated to facilitate the transport of nutrients to your muscles and the removal of waste products.
- **Injury Prevention:** Pay attention to your body and address any signs of overuse or injury promptly. Ignoring these warning signs can hinder your progress and lead to more severe issues.
- **Periodic Deload Weeks:** Incorporate deload weeks into your program, during which you reduce the training volume and intensity. Deload weeks allow your body to recover fully and can prevent burnout and overtraining.

Customizing Your Workout Program

An effective workout program should be tailored to your individual goals, experience level, and preferences. Here's how to customize your program:

Define Your Goals

Identify your specific muscle-building goals. Do you want to increase muscle size, strength, or both? Having clear objectives will guide your exercise selection and program structure.

Assess Your Experience

Your experience level matters. Beginners should start with a well-rounded, full-body program to build a foundation, while intermediate and advanced individuals can benefit from split routines and periodization.

Plan Your Schedule

Consider your weekly schedule when designing your program. How many days per week can you commit to training? This will determine the frequency of your workouts.

Exercise Selection

Choose exercises that align with your goals and preferences. Include compound movements for overall development and isolation exercises to target specific areas.

Repetition and Set Schemes

Select the repetition and set schemes that match your goals. Remember that variation is essential to prevent plateaus and encourage muscle growth.

Periodization

Incorporate periodization into your program to ensure continued progress. Periodization can be as simple as dividing your training into phases with specific goals.

Rest and Recovery

Prioritize rest and recovery to maximize your muscle-building potential. Adequate sleep, nutrition, and hydration are key elements.

Monitor Progress

Track your progress by recording your workouts, measuring your strength gains, and periodically reassessing your goals. Adapt your program as needed based on your progress.

Conclusion

Effective workout programming is the art of strategically structuring your training to maximize muscle growth while minimizing the risk of injury and burnout. The principles of progressive overload, exercise selection, repetition and set schemes, split routines, and periodization are your tools for sculpting a powerful physique.

As you embark on your muscle-building journey, remember that patience, consistency, and dedication are your allies. Your body is a masterpiece in progress, and with the right program, you have the power to shape it according to your vision. Continue your pursuit of excellence, and let the art of muscle building be your guide to success.

5. PROGRESSIVE OVERLOAD TECHNIQUES

Progressive overload is the heart and soul of muscle building. It's the principle that drives your muscles to grow stronger and larger over time. The essence of progressive overload is simple: you must gradually increase the demands on your muscles to elicit growth. In this comprehensive guide, we'll explore various progressive overload techniques that can supercharge your muscle-building journey and help you sculpt the physique you desire.

The Core Principle: What Is Progressive Overload?

At its core, progressive overload involves challenging your muscles with a workload that's greater than what they're accustomed to. It's about pushing your limits, setting new goals, and constantly striving for improvement. When you consistently apply progressive overload to your training, your body adapts by making your muscles bigger and stronger.

Progressive overload is the key to making continuous gains in muscle size, strength, and endurance. Without it, your progress can stagnate, and you may find yourself stuck on a plateau. To avoid hitting a wall in your training, you need to understand and apply a variety of progressive overload techniques.

1. Increasing Weight

The most straightforward way to apply progressive overload is to increase the weight you lift. Lifting heavier weights places a greater demand on your muscles, forcing them to adapt and grow. Here's how to effectively increase the weight in your workouts:

- **Incremental Increases:** Gradually add more weight to your exercises. For example, if you're currently lifting 50 pounds in a particular exercise, aim to lift 55 or 60 pounds in your next workout.
- **Lifting to Failure:** When you can comfortably perform the target number of repetitions with a specific weight, consider increasing the weight until you reach muscle failure within the desired rep range.
- **Microloading:** In some cases, you might find that adding the smallest standard increment (e.g., 5 pounds) is too challenging. In such situations, you can use fractional plates or magnetic microplates to make smaller weight increases.
- **Lifting in Percentage Increments:** Another approach is to increase the weight as a percentage of your one-repetition maximum (1RM). For instance, you might increase the weight by 2.5% or 5% in each workout.

2. Manipulating Repetition and Set Schemes

Varying the number of repetitions and sets in your workouts is a versatile way to apply progressive overload. Here are some strategies to consider:

- **Adding Repetitions:** Increase the number of repetitions you perform with a given weight. For instance, if you've been doing 3 sets of 8 reps with a particular weight, try doing 3 sets of 10 or 12 reps with the same weight.
- **Adding Sets:** Another approach is to add more sets to your workout. If you typically do 3 sets of an exercise, try doing 4 or 5 sets to increase the overall volume and workload.
- **Pyramid Sets:** Incorporate pyramid sets, where you gradually increase or decrease the weight and repetitions in successive sets. This variation can challenge your muscles differently and promote growth.
- **Reducing Rest Periods:** Shortening the rest periods between sets can increase the intensity of your workouts, making them

more demanding and promoting muscle growth.

3. Tempo Manipulation

Tempo refers to the speed at which you perform each repetition of an exercise. By altering the tempo, you can make your workouts more challenging and apply progressive overload effectively. Here are some tempo manipulation techniques:

- **Eccentric Emphasis:** Slow down the eccentric (muscle-lengthening) phase of the repetition. For example, take 3-4 seconds to lower the weight during a bench press. This increased time under tension can stimulate muscle growth.
- **Isometric Holds:** Introduce isometric holds at various points in the range of motion. For instance, pause for 2-3 seconds at the bottom of a squat or during the midpoint of a bicep curl.
- **Fast Explosive Repetitions:** Incorporate fast explosive repetitions during your sets. Explosive concentric (muscle-shortening) movements can recruit more muscle fibers and promote strength and power gains.

4. Increasing Training Frequency

Training frequency refers to how often you work a specific muscle group in a given period. Manipulating training frequency can be an effective way to apply progressive overload:

- **Increasing Weekly Workouts:** If you've been training a muscle group once a week, consider increasing the frequency to twice a week. This allows you to distribute the workload and accumulate more training volume.
- **Higher Frequency of Specific Exercises:** You can also increase the frequency of specific exercises within your workouts. For example, if you're working on your chest, you can add a second bench press session during the week.
- **Alternating Exercises:** Rotate between different exercises targeting the same muscle group. For instance, alternate

between barbell and dumbbell bench presses to introduce variety and progression.

5. Modifying Range of Motion

Manipulating the range of motion in your exercises can change how your muscles are engaged and add a new dimension to your training:

- **Partial Repetitions:** Incorporate partial repetitions by working within a specific range of motion. For example, you can focus on the upper half of a squat or the top portion of a pull-up for a few sets.
- **Full Range of Motion:** Ensure that you're performing exercises through their full range of motion. This emphasizes muscle engagement throughout the complete movement and can help you reach new levels of strength and muscle development.
- **Lunges:** Implement lunges and split squats, which involve a deeper range of motion than traditional squats, to challenge your leg muscles differently.

6. Incorporating Advanced Techniques

As you advance in your training, consider incorporating more advanced progressive overload techniques:

- **Drop Sets:** After completing a set with a challenging weight, immediately reduce the weight and perform additional repetitions. This intensifies the workout and exhausts your muscles for greater growth stimulus.
- **Supersets:** Supersets involve performing two exercises back-to-back without rest. This technique increases the training density and can stimulate muscle growth.
- **Negatives:** Negative repetitions involve focusing on the eccentric (muscle-lengthening) phase of the exercise. Lift a heavier weight during the concentric phase and slowly lower it during the eccentric phase.

- **Rest-Pause Sets:** After reaching muscle failure in a set, briefly rest (typically for 10-15 seconds) and then continue with additional repetitions. Rest-pause sets allow you to squeeze out more work in a single set.

7. Volume Manipulation

Volume is a key aspect of progressive overload. It refers to the total amount of work you do in your workout, usually calculated as sets multiplied by repetitions. Increasing training volume can drive muscle growth:

- **More Sets and Repetitions:** Increase the total number of sets and repetitions in your workouts to accumulate more training volume.
- **Volume Blocks:** Periodically focus on higher training volume blocks where you aim to do more sets and repetitions for specific muscle groups or exercises.
- **Density Training:** Density training involves performing a high number of sets and repetitions in a shorter amount of time. This can increase training density and promote growth.

8. Implementing Deload Weeks

Deload weeks are planned periods of reduced intensity and volume. While it may seem counterintuitive, incorporating deload weeks is a smart strategy in progressive overload:

- **Reduced Intensity:** During deload weeks, reduce the intensity of your workouts by using lighter weights and fewer sets and repetitions.
- **Active Recovery:** Use deload weeks as an opportunity for active recovery. Focus on mobility work, flexibility, and light cardio to promote recovery without overloading your muscles.
- **Preventing Overtraining:** Deload weeks can help prevent overtraining and injuries by giving your body and central nervous system time to recover fully.

9. Tracking and Monitoring

To apply progressive overload effectively, it's essential to track and monitor your progress. Here's how to do it:

- **Training Journal:** Maintain a training journal where you record each workout, including the exercises, sets, repetitions, and weights used.
- **Strength Logs:** Keep a log of your strength gains in key exercises. This will help you identify trends and set new goals for progressive overload.
- **Visual Progress:** Take photos of your physique regularly to visually track your muscle-building progress.
- **Performance Metrics:** Monitor performance metrics such as endurance, speed, and flexibility to ensure well-rounded progress in your training.

The Art of Balancing Progressive Overload

While applying progressive overload is essential for muscle growth, it's equally important to find the right balance. Overloading your muscles excessively can lead to overtraining, injuries, and burnout. To maintain a balanced approach to progressive overload:

- **Listen to Your Body:** Pay attention to your body's signals. If you're experiencing persistent fatigue, decreased performance, or signs of overuse injuries, it may be time for a lighter week or a deload period.
- **Set Realistic Goals:** Ensure that your progressive overload goals are achievable within a reasonable time frame. Unrealistic goals can lead to frustration and potential overtraining.
- **Rotate Techniques:** Don't rely on a single progressive overload technique exclusively. Rotate and combine different methods to prevent monotony and overuse.
- **Recovery and Nutrition:** Prioritize recovery and nutrition to support the demands of progressive overload. Proper sleep,

nutrition, and hydration are vital for your muscles to recover and grow.
- **Seek Professional Guidance:** Consider consulting a fitness professional or personal trainer to help you design a balanced and effective progressive overload plan tailored to your goals and needs.

Conclusion

Progressive overload is the guiding principle that propels your muscle-building journey forward. By understanding and applying various progressive overload techniques, you can continually challenge your muscles, break through plateaus, and achieve the strength and physique you desire. Remember that progressive overload is both an art and a science, and its mastery is a key to your success in the art of muscle building.

6. MAXIMIZING MUSCLE HYPERTROPHY

Muscle hypertrophy, the process of increasing the size and volume of your muscle cells, is at the heart of the art of muscle building. Whether you're aiming for a sculpted physique, enhanced performance, or improved overall health, maximizing muscle hypertrophy is key. In this comprehensive guide, we'll delve into the science and strategies behind muscle growth, providing you with the tools and knowledge to sculpt your ideal physique.

Understanding Muscle Hypertrophy

Before diving into the strategies for maximizing muscle hypertrophy, it's essential to understand the science behind it. Muscle hypertrophy occurs as a result of two main types of adaptations: myofibrillar hypertrophy and sarcoplasmic hypertrophy.

1. Myofibrillar Hypertrophy

Myofibrillar hypertrophy involves an increase in the size and number of myofibrils, which are the contractile proteins within muscle cells. This type of hypertrophy primarily contributes to strength gains and is characterized by dense, compact muscle tissue. Training with heavier weights and lower repetitions typically stimulates myofibrillar hypertrophy.

2. Sarcoplasmic Hypertrophy

Sarcoplasmic hypertrophy, on the other hand, is an increase in the volume of the sarcoplasm, the fluid and energy-rich gel-like substance that surrounds the myofibrils within muscle cells. This type of hypertrophy leads to larger, more voluminous muscles. Training with moderate to high repetitions and shorter rest intervals often stimulates sarcoplasmic hypertrophy.

To maximize muscle hypertrophy, it's crucial to understand that both types play a role in overall muscle growth. The strategies you implement should strike a balance to achieve well-rounded development.

The Science of Muscle Growth

To promote muscle hypertrophy, you need to grasp the physiological processes at work. Muscle growth primarily occurs through a process known as muscle protein synthesis (MPS) and muscle protein breakdown (MPB).

Muscle Protein Synthesis (MPS)

MPS is the creation of new muscle proteins, a process that leads to muscle growth and repair. To stimulate MPS, your body needs to be in an anabolic state, where the rate of protein synthesis exceeds the rate of protein breakdown.

Several factors can influence MPS:

- **Resistance Training:** Engaging in resistance training, particularly with challenging loads, is a potent stimulator of MPS.
- **Protein Intake:** Consuming adequate protein, which provides essential amino acids, is crucial for muscle protein synthesis.
- **Hormonal Response:** Hormones like testosterone and growth hormone play a role in MPS, with resistance training and adequate nutrition supporting their release.

Muscle Protein Breakdown (MPB)

MPB is the process of breaking down muscle proteins. While some level of MPB is normal and necessary for muscle remodeling, excessive MPB can hinder muscle growth.

Several factors can influence MPB:

- **Catabolic Hormones:** Hormones like cortisol can increase MPB when elevated. Stress management is essential to control catabolic hormone levels.
- **Excessive Exercise:** Overtraining and excessive exercise without adequate recovery can increase MPB.
- **Inadequate Nutrition:** A lack of protein or calories can increase the rate of muscle protein breakdown.

Balancing MPS and MPB is vital for promoting muscle hypertrophy. By strategically implementing training, nutrition, and recovery strategies, you can tip the scale in favor of muscle growth.

Nutrition for Muscle Hypertrophy

Nutrition is a cornerstone of muscle hypertrophy. To maximize muscle growth, you need to provide your body with the essential building blocks, energy, and recovery support. Here are key nutritional considerations for muscle hypertrophy:

Protein

Protein is the fundamental macronutrient for muscle hypertrophy. It provides the amino acids necessary for muscle repair and growth. To support muscle hypertrophy, consider the following protein-related strategies:

- **Adequate Protein Intake:** Aim to consume enough protein to meet your daily requirements. A common recommendation is 1.6 to 2.2 grams of protein per kilogram of body weight.
- **Protein Timing:** Distribute your protein intake throughout the day, with a focus on post-workout protein to support recovery and muscle growth.
- **Quality Protein Sources:** Opt for high-quality protein sources, including lean meats, fish, eggs, dairy, and plant-based options like legumes, tofu, and tempeh.

Calories

To promote muscle hypertrophy, you need to be in a caloric surplus, where you consume more calories than your body expends. This surplus provides the energy required for muscle growth. Consider the following calorie-related strategies:

- **Caloric Surplus:** Calculate your daily caloric needs and aim for a modest surplus. Excessive calorie intake can lead to unwanted fat gain.
- **Balanced Macronutrients:** Ensure that your surplus includes a balanced distribution of macronutrients, with an emphasis on protein for muscle growth.

Micronutrients

Micronutrients, including vitamins and minerals, are essential for overall health and indirectly support muscle growth. Ensuring you have a balanced intake of vitamins and minerals through a diverse diet is crucial for muscle hypertrophy.

Hydration

Proper hydration is vital for muscle function and overall health. Dehydration can lead to decreased exercise performance and hinder muscle recovery. Ensure you stay adequately hydrated.

Resistance Training for Muscle Hypertrophy

Resistance training, whether using free weights, machines, or bodyweight exercises, is the primary stimulus for muscle hypertrophy. To maximize the effectiveness of your resistance training, consider the following strategies:

Exercise Selection

Choose exercises that target the muscle groups you want to develop. A combination of compound (multi-joint) and isolation (single-joint) exercises can provide a well-rounded approach to muscle growth.

Progressive Overload

As mentioned earlier, progressive overload is the principle of gradually increasing the demands on your muscles. This can be achieved by increasing the weight, adjusting the repetition and set schemes, manipulating tempo, and altering other training variables.

Volume and Frequency

Training volume, calculated as sets multiplied by repetitions, plays a significant role in muscle hypertrophy. Performing multiple sets with moderate to high repetitions can stimulate sarcoplasmic hypertrophy.

Training frequency is the number of times you work a specific muscle group in a week. Higher training frequency can be beneficial for maximizing muscle hypertrophy. Split routines, full-body workouts, and periodization can help structure your training.

Rest and Recovery

Adequate rest and recovery are essential for muscle growth. Ensure that you get sufficient sleep, allow muscles to recover between workouts, and address any signs of overuse or injury promptly.

Recovery and Regeneration

Recovery is a crucial, often underestimated aspect of muscle hypertrophy. Focusing on recovery strategies can help you bounce back from intense workouts, prevent overtraining, and support muscle growth. Here are key recovery and regeneration strategies:

Sleep

Sleep is the primary time for your body to recover and grow. Aim for 7-9 hours of quality sleep per night to support muscle hypertrophy.

Nutrition

Post-workout nutrition is essential to support muscle recovery and growth. Consume a post-workout meal or shake rich in protein and carbohydrates to replenish glycogen stores and promote muscle repair.

Active Recovery

Incorporate active recovery strategies like light cardio, yoga, or mobility work on your rest days to maintain flexibility and circulation.

Foam Rolling and Stretching

Foam rolling and stretching can help alleviate muscle tightness and reduce the risk of injury. Spend time on mobility work to maintain muscle health.

Massage and Bodywork

Professional massages and bodywork can help release muscle tension, improve circulation, and support muscle recovery. Consider periodic massages to aid in recovery.

Stress Management

Stress management is essential to control catabolic hormones that can increase muscle protein breakdown. Techniques like meditation, deep breathing, and relaxation can help manage stress.

Periodic Deload Weeks

Incorporate deload weeks into your training program, during which you reduce the training volume and intensity. Deload weeks allow your body to recover fully and can prevent burnout and overtraining.

Periodization for Muscle Hypertrophy

Periodization is a systematic approach to structuring your training program. It involves dividing your training into specific cycles, each with its own goals and focus. Periodization helps prevent plateaus, minimizes overuse injuries, and ensures continued progress. Here are the three primary phases of periodization for muscle hypertrophy:

1. Hypertrophy Phase

The hypertrophy phase focuses on stimulating muscle growth through higher-repetition, moderate-weight training. It aims to increase muscle size and volume, particularly through sarcoplasmic hypertrophy.

2. Strength and Power Phase

The strength and power phase follows the hypertrophy phase and concentrates on building raw strength. This phase typically involves low-repetition, high-weight training to promote myofibrillar hypertrophy and strength gains.

3. Deload and Transition Phase

Periodization also includes deload and transition phases, during which you reduce training intensity and volume to promote recovery and prepare for the next phase.

Periodization can be adapted and personalized based on your experience level, goals, and the time you have available for training.

Common Mistakes and Pitfalls

While maximizing muscle hypertrophy requires dedication and effort, it's important to avoid common mistakes and pitfalls. Here are some pitfalls to watch out for:

Neglecting Progressive Overload

One of the most significant mistakes is neglecting progressive overload. Without continually increasing the demands on your muscles, you'll find it challenging to achieve optimal muscle growth.

Overtraining

Overtraining occurs when you don't allow sufficient recovery between workouts or when you perform excessive training volume. Overtraining can hinder muscle growth and lead to burnout and injury.

Inadequate Nutrition

Nutrition is a cornerstone of muscle hypertrophy. Inadequate protein intake, insufficient calories, and poor macronutrient balance can hinder your progress.

Lack of Periodization

Failing to implement a structured periodization plan can lead to plateaus and stagnation in your training.

Ignoring Recovery

Neglecting recovery strategies can hinder muscle growth and increase the risk of overuse injuries.

Unrealistic Expectations

Setting unrealistic goals for muscle hypertrophy can lead to frustration and disappointment. Understand that progress takes time and consistency.

Conclusion

Maximizing muscle hypertrophy is a multifaceted process that involves understanding the science of muscle growth, implementing effective resistance training, optimizing nutrition, prioritizing recovery and regeneration, and utilizing periodization strategies. To sculpt your ideal physique, you must become a master of the art of muscle building.

Consistency, dedication, and patience are your allies on this journey. By applying the knowledge and strategies outlined in this guide, you can unlock your full muscle-building potential and sculpt a physique that reflects the artistry of your hard work and dedication.

7. STRENGTH TRAINING PRINCIPLES

Strength training is the cornerstone of muscle building. It not only builds muscle but also enhances your performance, promotes overall health, and boosts your self-confidence. To master the art of muscle building, it's essential to understand the principles of strength training. In this comprehensive guide, we'll explore the science, strategies, and key principles that form the foundation of effective strength training.

The Science of Strength Training

Before delving into the principles of strength training, it's important to understand the underlying science. Strength training elicits adaptations in your muscles, nervous system, and connective tissues, ultimately leading to increased strength and muscle growth.

Muscle Hypertrophy

One of the primary adaptations from strength training is muscle hypertrophy, which is the growth and enlargement of muscle fibers. This occurs primarily through two mechanisms:

- **Myofibrillar Hypertrophy:** This involves an increase in the size and number of myofibrils, the contractile units within muscle fibers. Myofibrillar hypertrophy is associated with increased strength and denser muscle tissue.
- **Sarcoplasmic Hypertrophy:** Sarcoplasm is the gel-like substance that surrounds the myofibrils. Sarcoplasmic hypertrophy involves an increase in the volume of this fluid and is associated with larger, more voluminous muscles.

Balancing both types of hypertrophy is crucial for achieving well-rounded muscle development.

Neural Adaptations

Strength training also enhances the efficiency of your nervous system. Your body learns to recruit more motor units (a motor neuron and the muscle fibers it controls) to generate force. This adaptation results in increased strength without significant muscle growth, particularly in the initial stages of training.

Connective Tissue Strengthening

As you engage in strength training, your connective tissues, including tendons and ligaments, adapt to the increased load. These tissues become stronger and more resilient, reducing the risk of injuries.

The Principles of Strength Training

To make the most of your strength training efforts, you need to understand and apply the following key principles:

1. Progressive Overload

Progressive overload is the foundation of strength training. It involves continually increasing the demands on your muscles to stimulate growth and strength gains. This can be achieved by:

- **Increasing Weight:** Gradually lift heavier weights in your exercises over time.
- **Adding Repetitions:** Perform more repetitions with the same weight.
- **Adjusting Sets:** Increase the number of sets in your workouts.
- **Manipulating Tempo:** Change the speed at which you perform each repetition.
- **Reducing Rest Periods:** Shorten the rest intervals between sets and exercises.

The key is to consistently challenge your muscles with increased resistance, time under tension, or intensity.

2. Exercise Selection

Choosing the right exercises is crucial. Compound exercises involve multiple muscle groups and joints and are excellent for overall strength and muscle development. Examples include squats, deadlifts, bench presses, and pull-ups. Isolation exercises focus on specific muscle groups and can be used strategically to address weaknesses or aesthetic goals.

Your program should include a balance of both compound and isolation exercises to ensure comprehensive development.

3. Repetition and Set Schemes

The way you structure repetitions and sets plays a significant role in your strength training program. Different repetition and set schemes produce varying results:

- **Low Repetitions, High Weight:** This approach focuses on developing strength and power. For example, 4 sets of 4-6 repetitions with heavy weights are common.
- **Moderate Repetitions, Moderate Weight:** A popular choice for overall strength and muscle development is 3 sets of 8-12 repetitions with moderate weight.
- **High Repetitions, Low Weight:** Higher repetitions with lower weights are often used for endurance and hypertrophy. This approach may involve 3 sets of 15-20 repetitions.
- **Pyramid Sets:** Pyramid sets involve progressively increasing or decreasing the weight and repetitions in successive sets. This can be an effective way to challenge your muscles and stimulate growth.

4. Rest and Recovery

Adequate rest and recovery are essential for effective strength training. Pay attention to the following aspects:

- **Rest Days:** Incorporate rest days into your program to allow your muscles to recover and repair.

- **Sleep:** Aim for 7-9 hours of quality sleep per night, as this is when your body primarily repairs and grows muscle tissue.
- **Nutrition:** Support your recovery with proper nutrition, including a post-workout meal rich in protein and carbohydrates.
- **Hydration:** Stay hydrated to facilitate the transport of nutrients to your muscles and the removal of waste products.
- **Injury Prevention:** Address any signs of overuse or injury promptly to avoid hindering your progress and risking more severe issues.

5. Periodization

Periodization is a structured approach to planning your training. It involves dividing your training into specific cycles, each with its own goals and focus. Periodization helps prevent plateaus, minimizes overuse injuries, and ensures continued progress. Here are the primary phases of periodization:

- **Anatomical Adaptation Phase:** The focus is on building a solid foundation by targeting structural balance and muscular endurance.
- **Hypertrophy Phase:** This phase aims to stimulate muscle growth through higher repetitions and moderate-weight training.
- **Strength and Power Phase:** The goal is to maximize strength and power gains through low-repetition, high-weight training.

Periodization can be adapted and personalized based on your experience level, goals, and the time you have available for training.

6. Range of Motion

Performing exercises through their full range of motion is important for strength training. This engages muscles fully, encourages mobility, and reduces the risk of injury. Avoid shortening the range of motion, as this limits muscle activation and development.

7. Form and Technique

Proper form and technique are non-negotiable in strength training. Maintaining correct form reduces the risk of injury and ensures that the targeted muscles are worked effectively. Consider seeking guidance from a qualified fitness professional or trainer to learn and perfect your technique.

8. Consistency

Consistency is a fundamental principle of strength training. Results come from continuous effort over time. Stick to your training program, and avoid frequent changes that can hinder progress.

Structuring Your Strength Training Program

To apply the principles of strength training effectively, you need to structure your program. Here's a step-by-step guide to help you create a well-rounded training plan:

Define Your Goals

Start by identifying your specific goals. Do you want to focus on strength, hypertrophy, or a combination of both? Having clear objectives will guide your exercise selection and program structure.

Assess Your Experience

Your experience level matters. Beginners should start with a well-rounded, full-body program to build a foundation, while intermediate and advanced individuals can benefit from split routines and more advanced periodization.

Plan Your Schedule

Consider your weekly schedule when designing your program. How many days per week can you commit to training? This will determine the frequency of your workouts.

Exercise Selection

Choose exercises that align with your goals and preferences. Include compound movements for overall development and isolation exercises to target specific areas.

Repetition and Set Schemes

Select the repetition and set schemes that match your goals. Remember that variation is essential to prevent plateaus and encourage muscle growth.

Periodization

Incorporate periodization into your program to ensure continued progress. Periodization can be as simple as dividing your training into phases with specific goals.

Rest and Recovery

Prioritize rest and recovery to maximize your strength-building potential. Adequate sleep, nutrition, and hydration are key elements.

Monitor Progress

Track your progress by recording your workouts, measuring your strength gains, and periodically reassessing your goals. Adapt your program as needed based on your progress.

Common Mistakes and Pitfalls

While the principles of strength training are straightforward, there are common mistakes and pitfalls to avoid:

- **Overtraining:** Excessive training volume or insufficient recovery can lead to overtraining, hindering progress and increasing the risk of injuries.
- **Neglecting Nutrition:** Inadequate protein intake or a lack of calories can limit your strength gains and muscle growth.
- **Poor Form:** Neglecting proper form and technique can lead to injuries and reduce the effectiveness of your training.
- **Inconsistent Training:** Consistency is key. Frequent program changes can hinder progress and prevent you from fully benefiting from your training.
- **Ignoring Periodization:** A lack of structured planning can result in plateaus and stagnation.
- **Neglecting Rest and Recovery:** Ignoring the need for rest and recovery can hinder strength gains and increase the risk of

overuse injuries.

Conclusion

Strength training is a dynamic and artful process that involves understanding the science, applying the principles, and structuring your program effectively. By mastering these principles, you can harness the full potential of your body, build strength, and sculpt your ideal physique. Whether you're a beginner or an experienced lifter, the art of muscle building begins with a strong foundation of strength training. Stay consistent, stay dedicated, and let the principles of strength guide you toward success.

8. CARDIO AND CONDITIONING FOR MUSCLE BUILDERS

When it comes to muscle building, the focus is often on strength training and resistance exercises. However, the art of muscle building extends beyond just lifting weights. Cardiovascular fitness and conditioning play a crucial role in achieving a well-rounded and sculpted physique. In this comprehensive guide, we'll explore the importance of cardio and conditioning for muscle builders, how to strike the right balance, and the strategies to incorporate them effectively into your training regimen.

The Importance of Cardio and Conditioning

Cardiovascular fitness and conditioning, often referred to as "cardio," have a multitude of benefits for muscle builders:

1. Fat Loss

Cardio is an effective tool for shedding excess body fat. Engaging in cardio workouts helps create a calorie deficit, which is essential for losing fat and revealing the muscle definition you've worked hard to build.

2. Improved Endurance

Cardiovascular workouts improve your cardiovascular and respiratory systems. Enhanced endurance allows you to work harder and longer during strength training sessions, which can lead to greater muscle gains.

3. Enhanced Recovery

Cardio activities help improve circulation, which can aid in the recovery process. Increased blood flow brings more nutrients to the muscles and removes waste products, contributing to faster recovery.

4. Heart Health

A healthy cardiovascular system is crucial for overall health and longevity. Cardio workouts strengthen the heart, lower the risk of heart disease, and improve cholesterol levels.

5. Mental Toughness

Cardio workouts often require mental toughness and discipline. Building mental resilience in cardio training can translate into a stronger mindset for your strength training and overall fitness journey.

6. Balanced Physique

Including cardio in your routine can help create a more balanced physique. It can prevent excessive muscle bulk and add definition to your muscles.

Finding the Right Balance

The key to successful muscle building is striking the right balance between strength training and cardiovascular conditioning. Finding the optimal balance depends on your individual goals, body type, and preferences. Here's how to find the right equilibrium:

1. Define Your Goals

Start by clearly defining your goals. Are you primarily interested in gaining muscle size and strength, or do you want a balance of muscle development and cardiovascular fitness? Understanding your objectives will guide your training approach.

2. Assess Your Body Type

Consider your body type when determining the balance between strength training and cardio. Endomorphs, who tend to store more body fat, may need a more significant focus on cardio for fat loss. Ectomorphs, who struggle to gain weight, may benefit from more strength training.

3. Individual Preferences

Your personal preferences play a significant role. Some individuals enjoy cardiovascular activities and find them essential for their mental well-being, while others may prefer more time spent on strength training.

4. Periodization

Consider implementing periodization into your training program. Periodization involves dividing your training into specific cycles, each with its own goals and focus. For example, you can have strength-focused phases and conditioning-focused phases to ensure a well-rounded approach.

5. Experiment and Adapt

Don't be afraid to experiment with different ratios of strength training and cardio. Pay attention to how your body responds and adjust your training accordingly. Your ideal balance may change over time as your goals evolve.

Cardio Strategies for Muscle Builders

When incorporating cardio into your muscle-building routine, it's essential to choose the right types of cardio workouts and strategies. Here are some effective approaches:

1. High-Intensity Interval Training (HIIT)

HIIT is a cardio strategy that alternates short bursts of intense exercise with brief recovery periods. It's an efficient way to burn calories, improve endurance, and boost cardiovascular fitness while preserving muscle mass.

Sample HIIT Workout:

- Warm-up for 5 minutes with light jogging.
- Sprint at maximum effort for 30 seconds.
- Recover with 60 seconds of slow jogging or walking.
- Repeat the sprint/recovery cycle for 15-20 minutes.
- Cool down with 5 minutes of walking.

2. Steady-State Cardio

Steady-state cardio involves maintaining a consistent intensity throughout your workout. It's effective for improving cardiovascular fitness and can be less taxing on the body compared to HIIT.

Sample Steady-State Cardio Workout:

- Choose an activity like jogging, cycling, or swimming.
- Maintain a steady pace for 30-60 minutes.
- You should be able to hold a conversation while exercising.

3. Cardio Machines

Cardio machines like the treadmill, stationary bike, and elliptical offer controlled environments for cardiovascular workouts. These machines allow you to monitor and adjust the intensity, making them suitable for both steady-state cardio and HIIT.

4. Sports and Outdoor Activities

Engaging in sports or outdoor activities can make cardio more enjoyable. Activities like basketball, soccer, hiking, and swimming offer cardiovascular benefits while allowing you to have fun and socialize.

5. Group Classes

Group fitness classes, such as spinning, aerobic dance, or circuit training, offer structured and motivating cardio workouts. These classes can be an excellent way to break up the monotony of traditional cardio routines.

Conditioning Strategies for Muscle Builders

Conditioning exercises complement cardio by targeting specific aspects of fitness, such as agility, speed, power, and core strength. Incorporating conditioning workouts into your routine can enhance your overall athleticism and physical performance.

1. Plyometric Training

Plyometric exercises involve explosive movements that improve power and speed. Common plyometric exercises include box jumps, burpees, and jump squats.

Sample Plyometric Workout:

- Box Jumps: Perform 3 sets of 10-12 repetitions, jumping onto a sturdy box or platform.

2. Agility Drills

Agility drills are designed to improve your speed, quickness, and agility. They often involve lateral movements, quick changes of direction, and reaction drills.

Sample Agility Drill:

- Ladder Drills: Lay an agility ladder on the ground and perform various footwork patterns, such as side shuffles, high knees, and quick steps, for 15-20 minutes.

3. Sled Drags and Pushes

Sled workouts are fantastic for building strength and power, enhancing cardiovascular fitness, and developing functional strength.

Sample Sled Workout:

- Load a sled with weight plates.
- Perform sled pushes for 20-30 yards followed by a 30-second rest.
- Repeat for 6-8 sets.

4. Bodyweight Conditioning

Bodyweight exercises can be an excellent conditioning tool. Exercises like burpees, mountain climbers, and bear crawls provide a full-body workout and improve muscular endurance.

Sample Bodyweight Conditioning Workout:

- Perform 4 rounds of:
    - 20 burpees
    - 30 seconds of mountain climbers
    - 40 feet of bear crawls

5. CrossFit

CrossFit workouts combine elements of cardio, strength training, and conditioning. These high-intensity workouts are designed to improve all aspects of fitness and athleticism.

Combining Strength Training, Cardio, and Conditioning

Balancing strength training, cardio, and conditioning is essential to achieve your desired physique and fitness level. Here's how to combine these elements effectively in your training program:

1. Periodization

Incorporate periodization into your training plan to ensure that you have phases dedicated to strength, cardio, and conditioning. Periodization allows you to prioritize different aspects of fitness at various times.

For example, you might follow a program with the following phases:

- **Hypertrophy Phase:** Focus on muscle building with a mix of strength training and moderate-intensity cardio.
- **Strength Phase:** Prioritize strength gains with heavy resistance training and minimal cardio.
- **Conditioning Phase:** Shift your focus to cardio and conditioning workouts to improve cardiovascular fitness and athleticism.

2. Hybrid Workouts

Combine strength training and conditioning into a single session to save time and maximize efficiency. For example, you can perform a circuit that includes both strength exercises and conditioning drills, such as kettlebell swings, battle ropes, and bodyweight movements.

Sample Hybrid Workout:

- Complete 3 rounds of:
    - Deadlifts: 8 repetitions
    - Kettlebell Swings: 15 repetitions
    - Push-Ups: 12 repetitions
    - Battle Ropes: 30 seconds

3. Alternate Days

Another approach is to alternate between strength training days and cardio/conditioning days. This method provides sufficient recovery time for each aspect of your training.

Sample Weekly Schedule:

- Monday: Strength Training
- Tuesday: Cardio/Conditioning
- Wednesday: Rest or Active Recovery
- Thursday: Strength Training
- Friday: Cardio/Conditioning
- Saturday: Rest or Active Recovery
- Sunday: Rest

4. Morning Cardio

Incorporate low-intensity morning cardio sessions on your rest days or after strength training. This can help with fat loss, improve cardiovascular fitness, and enhance recovery.

5. Monitor Your Progress

Keep a training journal to monitor your progress in both strength training and cardio/conditioning. Track your weights lifted, exercise times, distances covered, and any personal bests. Regular assessment helps you adjust your program as needed.

Common Mistakes and Pitfalls

When incorporating cardio and conditioning into your muscle-building regimen, it's important to avoid common mistakes that can hinder your progress:

- **Overemphasis on Cardio:** Spending too much time on cardio at the expense of strength training can limit muscle growth.
- **Inadequate Recovery:** Neglecting rest and recovery can lead to overtraining and hinder your muscle-building efforts.

- **Excessive High-Intensity Cardio:** Doing too much high-intensity cardio, especially on top of intense strength training, can lead to burnout and overtraining.
- **Ignoring Nutrition:** Failing to adjust your nutrition to accommodate increased activity levels can limit your muscle-building potential.
- **Lack of Variety:** Repeating the same cardio and conditioning routines without variety can lead to plateaus and boredom.

Conclusion

Cardio and conditioning are integral components of the art of muscle building. They help you achieve a balanced and well-rounded physique, improve cardiovascular fitness, and support overall health. Finding the right balance between strength training, cardio, and conditioning is essential, and it should align with your goals and preferences.

Remember that there is no one-size-fits-all approach to incorporating cardio and conditioning into your muscle-building routine. Experiment, adapt, and stay consistent with your training to optimize your results. Whether you're a bodybuilder, powerlifter, or fitness enthusiast, a well-rounded approach that includes both strength and cardiovascular conditioning is the key to achieving your fitness and physique goals.

9. RECOVERY AND REST DAYS

The pursuit of a sculpted and muscular physique is a journey that requires dedication, hard work, and discipline. While the focus is often on intense workouts and proper nutrition, one aspect that is frequently overlooked but equally crucial is recovery and rest days. In the art of muscle building, the ability to recover effectively and incorporate well-planned rest days into your routine can make a significant difference in your progress and overall success. In this comprehensive guide, we'll explore the science and strategies behind recovery and rest, helping you understand their importance and how to master them for optimal muscle building.

The Significance of Recovery and Rest

To appreciate the importance of recovery and rest, it's essential to understand their roles in the muscle-building process:

1. Muscle Repair and Growth

Intense resistance training creates microscopic damage to muscle fibers. During the recovery process, these damaged fibers are repaired and, in the presence of proper nutrition, become stronger and larger. Adequate recovery ensures that this repair process is optimized, leading to muscle growth.

2. Energy Restoration

Exercising, especially strength training, depletes energy stores in your muscles and liver. Proper recovery allows your body to replenish these energy stores, ensuring you have the necessary fuel for subsequent workouts.

3. Central Nervous System Recovery

Strength training, in particular, places a significant demand on your central nervous system. Recovery is crucial for your nervous system to recuperate and function optimally, allowing you to continue lifting heavy weights with proper form and intensity.

4. Hormonal Balance

Hormones play a pivotal role in muscle building. Adequate rest, particularly sleep, helps maintain hormonal balance, including the production of growth hormone and testosterone, which are essential for muscle growth.

5. Injury Prevention

Recovery and rest allow your body to heal and prevent overuse injuries. Ignoring the need for recovery can lead to overtraining and an increased risk of muscular strains, joint issues, and other injuries.

6. Psychological Rejuvenation

The mental aspect of muscle building should not be underestimated. Adequate recovery and rest help reduce mental fatigue, stress, and burnout. A refreshed mindset can positively impact your motivation and commitment to your training.

7. Longevity

Prioritizing recovery and rest is essential for long-term progress and overall health. It helps prevent burnout and overtraining, allowing you to maintain a consistent training regimen over the years.

The Science of Recovery

Effective recovery is rooted in the science of how the body responds to exercise and the factors that influence the process. Here are some key principles of recovery:

1. Muscle Protein Synthesis (MPS)

MPS is the process through which your body repairs and builds new muscle tissue. It's stimulated by resistance training and proper nutrition. Maximizing MPS is essential for muscle growth, and it primarily occurs during the recovery period after workouts.

2. Hormonal Balance

Hormones like testosterone, growth hormone, and insulin-like growth factor (IGF-1) play a critical role in muscle building. Proper recovery, including sleep and nutrition, supports the production and regulation of these anabolic hormones.

3. Nutrient Timing

The timing of your meals and nutrient intake is crucial for recovery. Consuming a post-workout meal that includes protein and carbohydrates helps replenish glycogen stores, promotes muscle repair, and initiates the recovery process.

4. Hydration

Proper hydration is essential for overall health and effective recovery. Dehydration can lead to decreased exercise performance and hinder muscle repair and growth.

5. Sleep

Sleep is when your body primarily repairs and grows muscle tissue. Aim for 7-9 hours of quality sleep per night to support muscle-building efforts.

6. Active Recovery

Incorporating light activity on rest days, known as active recovery, can help maintain circulation, alleviate muscle soreness, and enhance recovery. Activities like walking, yoga, or swimming are ideal for active recovery.

Strategies for Effective Recovery

Now that we've covered the science behind recovery, it's time to explore the strategies for enhancing your recovery process:

1. Proper Nutrition

Nutrition is a cornerstone of effective recovery. To optimize muscle building and recovery, consider the following nutritional strategies:

- **Protein Intake:** Consume an adequate amount of high-quality protein to provide essential amino acids necessary for muscle repair and growth. A common recommendation is 1.6 to 2.2 grams of protein per kilogram of body weight.
- **Carbohydrate Intake:** Carbohydrates replenish glycogen stores, which are essential for energy and recovery. Include carbohydrates in your post-workout meal or shake.
- **Healthy Fats:** Incorporate healthy fats like avocados, nuts, and olive oil into your diet to support overall health and inflammation control.
- **Micronutrients:** Ensure you receive a balanced intake of vitamins and minerals through a diverse diet or supplementation. Micronutrients are essential for muscle health and overall recovery.
- **Hydration:** Stay adequately hydrated by drinking water throughout the day. Proper hydration supports digestion, nutrient transport, and waste removal.
- **Post-Workout Nutrition:** Consume a post-workout meal or shake rich in protein and carbohydrates within a few hours after your training session to promote muscle repair and recovery.

2. Sleep

Quality sleep is essential for recovery and muscle building. Consider these strategies to improve your sleep quality:

- **Consistent Sleep Schedule:** Go to bed and wake up at the same time each day, even on weekends, to regulate your body's internal clock.
- **Dark and Cool Room:** Create a sleep-conducive environment by keeping your bedroom dark, quiet, and at a comfortable temperature.
- **Limit Screen Time:** Reduce exposure to screens, such as phones and computers, before bedtime. The blue light emitted from screens can disrupt sleep patterns.

- **Bedtime Routine:** Establish a relaxing bedtime routine to signal to your body that it's time to wind down. This might include reading, taking a warm bath, or practicing relaxation techniques.
- **Limit Caffeine and Alcohol:** Avoid consuming caffeine and alcohol close to bedtime, as they can interfere with sleep.

3. Active Recovery

Incorporate active recovery into your routine to maintain circulation, alleviate muscle soreness, and promote relaxation. Consider the following active recovery strategies:

- **Walking:** Go for a leisurely walk to keep your body moving without adding stress to your muscles.
- **Yoga:** Yoga can help improve flexibility, reduce muscle tension, and promote relaxation.
- **Swimming:** Swimming is a low-impact, full-body exercise that can be an excellent choice for active recovery.
- **Foam Rolling and Stretching:** Use a foam roller to release muscle tightness and perform static stretching to improve flexibility.
- **Light Cardio:** Engage in light cardiovascular activities like cycling or elliptical training at a low intensity.

4. Stress Management

Stress management is crucial for effective recovery. High levels of stress can increase the production of catabolic hormones that break down muscle tissue. Consider these stress management techniques:

- **Meditation:** Regular meditation practice can help reduce stress and promote relaxation.
- **Deep Breathing:** Deep breathing exercises can calm the nervous system and reduce stress.
- **Progressive Muscle Relaxation:** This technique involves tensing and then releasing muscle groups to promote physical

and mental relaxation.
- **Time Management:** Effective time management can help reduce the stress associated with a busy lifestyle. Prioritize tasks and create a balanced schedule.

5. Periodic Deload Weeks

Incorporate deload weeks into your training program. A deload week involves reducing training volume and intensity to allow your body to recover fully. Deload weeks can prevent burnout and overtraining.

6. Massage and Bodywork

Professional massages and bodywork can help release muscle tension, improve circulation, and support muscle recovery. Consider periodic massages to aid in recovery.

Rest Days: The Art of Active Rest

Rest days are a critical component of recovery. However, rest doesn't necessarily mean complete inactivity. Active rest days involve light physical activity that promotes recovery without causing additional strain on the muscles. Here's how to make the most of your rest days:

1. Active Recovery Workouts

Consider incorporating active recovery workouts on your rest days. These workouts should be low-intensity and focus on flexibility, mobility, and relaxation. Activities like yoga, Pilates, or light swimming are ideal for active recovery.

2. Mobility and Stretching

Dedicate time to mobility exercises and stretching on your rest days. This can help alleviate muscle tightness, improve joint range of motion, and prevent injuries.

3. Walking

A leisurely walk is a simple and effective way to engage in active rest. Walking promotes blood circulation, relaxation, and mental clarity.

4. Light Cardio

Engage in light cardiovascular activities like cycling or low-intensity elliptical training. Keep the intensity low to avoid taxing your muscles.

5. Nutrition

Pay attention to your nutrition on rest days. While you may not need as many calories as on training days, it's important to maintain a balanced diet that supports recovery.

6. Hydration

Stay adequately hydrated on rest days to facilitate the removal of waste products and the transport of nutrients to your muscles.

7. Mental Rejuvenation

Use rest days as an opportunity to relax and recharge mentally. Engage in activities that promote mental well-being, such as reading, spending time with loved ones, or practicing mindfulness.

The Common Pitfalls of Recovery and Rest

While the science and strategies behind recovery and rest are well-established, there are common pitfalls to avoid:

- **Neglecting Sleep:** Inadequate sleep can hinder the recovery process and lead to overtraining.
- **Overtraining:** Pushing yourself too hard without allowing sufficient recovery can lead to overtraining, which can hinder progress and increase the risk of injury.
- **Inadequate Nutrition:** Failing to adjust your diet to support increased activity levels can limit your muscle-building potential.
- **Excessive Stress:** High levels of stress can increase the production of catabolic hormones, which can break down muscle tissue.
- **Inconsistent Recovery:** Inconsistent recovery strategies can hinder progress and lead to burnout.

- **Ignoring Rest Days:** Neglecting rest days can lead to overtraining, reduced muscle growth, and increased injury risk.

Conclusion

Recovery and rest are integral components of the art of muscle building. They are not signs of weakness but rather pillars of success. By understanding the science behind recovery and implementing effective strategies, you can optimize your muscle-building progress, prevent injuries, and promote overall health.

Remember that the journey to building a sculpted and muscular physique is a marathon, not a sprint. It's essential to prioritize recovery and incorporate well-planned rest days into your routine. The art of muscle building lies in mastering the delicate balance of pushing your body to its limits in the gym and allowing it to recover and rejuvenate, ultimately creating a masterpiece of strength, vitality, and well-being.

10. SUPPLEMENTS FOR MUSCLE ENHANCEMENT

The world of muscle building is a realm filled with dedication, sweat, and hard work. To many, the path to a chiseled physique is paved with countless hours in the gym and meticulous attention to nutrition. However, for those who are willing to explore the boundaries of muscle enhancement, supplements present an intriguing possibility. In the art of muscle building, supplements are tools that, when used judiciously and knowledgeably, can offer that extra edge, accelerating your journey towards your dream physique. In this comprehensive guide, we delve deep into the world of supplements for muscle enhancement, exploring the science behind them, the different types available, and how to use them effectively to unlock your full potential.

The Role of Supplements in Muscle Building

Before diving into the specifics of supplements for muscle enhancement, it's essential to understand their role in your fitness journey. Supplements should be viewed as precisely that – supplements to your diet and training regimen. They are not a magic pill that will instantly transform your physique, but rather tools to assist you in your quest for muscle growth.

Supplements can:

1. **Fill Nutritional Gaps:** Despite your best efforts, it can be challenging to get all the necessary nutrients through your diet alone. Supplements can help bridge the nutritional gaps and ensure you're not deficient in essential vitamins and minerals.

2. **Enhance Recovery:** Certain supplements can aid in the recovery process by reducing muscle soreness and speeding up muscle repair, allowing you to train more frequently and effectively.
3. **Boost Performance:** Some supplements can improve your workout performance, allowing you to train harder, lift heavier, and achieve better results.
4. **Support Muscle Growth:** Specific supplements are designed to promote muscle growth, either by increasing protein synthesis, testosterone levels, or other mechanisms.
5. **Aid Fat Loss:** While the primary focus of muscle building is, of course, muscle growth, it's often beneficial to simultaneously reduce body fat to reveal the muscles beneath. Some supplements can help with fat loss.
6. **Provide Convenience:** Supplements can offer a convenient and quick way to meet your nutritional needs, especially for individuals with busy lifestyles.

The Science Behind Supplements for Muscle Building

Understanding the science behind muscle-enhancing supplements is crucial for making informed choices and avoiding misconceptions. Let's delve into some key scientific concepts:

1. Muscle Protein Synthesis (MPS)

MPS is the process through which your body repairs and builds new muscle tissue in response to resistance training. Supplements like protein and amino acids can promote MPS, which is essential for muscle growth.

2. Hormones

Hormones play a significant role in muscle building. Testosterone, human growth hormone (HGH), and insulin-like growth factor (IGF-1) are anabolic hormones that promote muscle growth. Some supplements aim to support the production and regulation of these hormones.

3. Muscle Recovery

The process of muscle recovery involves repairing the microscopic damage caused by resistance training. Supplements can aid recovery by reducing muscle soreness, inflammation, and oxidative stress, helping you bounce back faster and train more effectively.

4. Nutrient Timing

The timing of your nutrient intake is crucial for muscle building. Post-workout nutrition, for example, is a window of opportunity to replenish glycogen stores, initiate muscle repair, and promote recovery.

5. Cellular Signaling

Cellular signaling pathways in your body respond to various factors, including exercise and nutrition. Some supplements aim to influence these pathways to enhance muscle growth and recovery.

Types of Supplements for Muscle Enhancement

The supplement market is vast and varied, offering a plethora of options. It's important to understand the different types of supplements and their specific purposes. Here are some common categories:

1. Protein Supplements

Protein is the building block of muscle, and adequate protein intake is essential for muscle growth. Protein supplements come in various forms, including:

- **Whey Protein:** Fast-absorbing and rich in essential amino acids, making it an excellent choice for post-workout nutrition.
- **Casein Protein:** Slow-digesting protein that can provide a steady supply of amino acids over several hours, such as during sleep.
- **Plant-Based Proteins:** Options like pea, rice, and hemp protein are suitable for vegetarians and vegans.
- **Protein Blends:** Combinations of different protein sources for a balanced amino acid profile.

2. Branched-Chain Amino Acids (BCAAs)

BCAAs, including leucine, isoleucine, and valine, are essential amino acids that play a vital role in muscle protein synthesis. BCAA supplements can support muscle recovery and reduce muscle soreness.

3. Creatine

Creatine is one of the most researched and effective supplements for muscle building. It enhances performance and muscle growth by increasing your body's ability to produce energy during high-intensity, short-duration activities.

4. Beta-Alanine

Beta-alanine is an amino acid that can enhance muscular endurance. It helps buffer lactic acid buildup, allowing you to train at a higher intensity for longer periods.

5. L-Glutamine

Glutamine is an amino acid that plays a role in muscle recovery. It can reduce muscle soreness and support the immune system.

6. Pre-Workout Supplements

Pre-workout supplements typically contain a combination of ingredients, including caffeine, amino acids, and nitric oxide boosters. They are designed to improve energy, focus, and workout performance.

7. Post-Workout Supplements

Post-workout supplements often include protein and carbohydrates to promote recovery, muscle repair, and glycogen replenishment.

8. Testosterone Boosters

Testosterone boosters are designed to support the production of testosterone, a hormone that plays a significant role in muscle building and recovery.

9. Fat Burners

While not directly related to muscle growth, fat burners can aid in fat loss, helping to reveal the muscles you've been working hard to build.

10. Multivitamins and Minerals

Multivitamins and mineral supplements can help fill nutritional gaps in your diet, ensuring you get all the essential nutrients needed for muscle building and overall health.

11. Omega-3 Fatty Acids

Omega-3 supplements can reduce inflammation, improve cardiovascular health, and support overall well-being.

12. HMB (Beta-Hydroxy Beta-Methylbutyrate)

HMB is a metabolite of leucine, an essential amino acid. It may help reduce muscle protein breakdown and support muscle growth.

The Art of Effective Supplement Usage

Using supplements effectively requires careful consideration and a well-thought-out approach. Here are some key strategies for incorporating supplements into your muscle-building journey:

1. Assess Your Nutritional Needs

Before adding any supplements to your regimen, assess your nutritional needs. Are there specific deficiencies or gaps in your diet that need to be addressed? Work with a healthcare professional or nutritionist to identify your specific needs.

2. Prioritize Real Food

Supplements should complement, not replace, real food. Whole foods provide a wide array of nutrients and offer benefits beyond what supplements can provide. Make whole, unprocessed foods the foundation of your diet.

3. Research Thoroughly

Don't jump into supplement usage without proper research. Understand the science behind each supplement, its potential benefits, and any side effects or risks. Look for reliable sources of information and consult with a healthcare professional if needed.

4. Quality Matters

Not all supplements are created equal. Quality can vary between brands and products. Opt for reputable, well-established companies with third-party testing and certifications to ensure product purity and accuracy.

5. Follow Recommended Dosages

Stick to the recommended dosages provided on the supplement labels. Consuming excessive amounts of certain supplements can be harmful and counterproductive.

6. Experiment Cautiously

Introduce supplements one at a time, and monitor how your body responds. Some supplements may work well for you, while others may not produce the desired effects.

7. Keep a Journal

Maintain a journal to track your supplement usage, diet, and workout performance. This can help you assess the impact of supplements on your progress and make necessary adjustments.

8. Consider Cycling

Some supplements, such as creatine, may benefit from cycling. Cycling involves periods of use followed by periods of abstinence to prevent desensitization to the supplement's effects.

9. Stay Hydrated

Many supplements can be dehydrating, so ensure you maintain adequate hydration throughout your training and supplement regimen.

10. Be Patient

Muscle building is a long-term endeavor, and supplements are not a quick fix. Be patient and consistent with your supplement usage, diet, and training to see meaningful results.

11. Listen to Your Body

Pay attention to how your body reacts to supplements. If you experience adverse effects or discomfort, discontinue use and consult with a healthcare professional.

Common Misconceptions and Pitfalls

In the world of supplements, several misconceptions and pitfalls should be avoided:

- **Magic Bullet Mentality:** Supplements are not a substitute for a well-structured training program and a balanced diet. They are meant to complement your efforts.
- **Overreliance on Supplements:** Relying solely on supplements while neglecting real food can lead to nutritional deficiencies and hinder overall health.
- **Uncritical Trust:** Blindly trusting supplement claims without proper research can lead to wasted money and potentially harmful effects.
- **Neglecting Whole Foods:** Supplements should not be used as a shortcut to avoid consuming whole foods. Real food provides a wide range of nutrients and health benefits that supplements cannot replicate.
- **Assuming Universal Benefits:** What works for one person may not work for another. Your individual needs and responses to supplements may differ, so it's essential to experiment and find what works best for you.

Conclusion

Supplements for muscle enhancement are tools that can offer advantages when used judiciously and knowledgeably. They are not a replacement for hard work, dedication, and a well-balanced diet but can be a valuable addition to your muscle-building journey.

To unlock the full potential of supplements, approach their usage with a clear understanding of the science behind them, an informed selection of products, and a careful, strategic integration into your diet and training regimen. Supplements, when used thoughtfully, can be the brushstrokes that add depth and detail to your masterpiece, allowing you to sculpt the body you've been striving to achieve in the art of muscle building.

11. INJURY PREVENTION AND MANAGEMENT

The art of muscle building is a testament to human determination and physical mastery. It's a journey of sculpting one's physique into a work of art, a living canvas showcasing the dedication and hard work of the individual. Yet, along this path, the risk of injury looms like an ever-present shadow, threatening to derail progress and stifle the pursuit of perfection. In this comprehensive guide, we will explore the essential principles of injury prevention and management, equipping you with the knowledge and strategies to safeguard your journey and achieve muscle mastery.

The Importance of Injury Prevention

Before delving into the specifics of injury prevention and management, it's crucial to understand why injury prevention is paramount in the realm of muscle building. Injuries can set you back in various ways, including:

1. **Disrupted Progress:** Injuries can halt your training and delay your progress, making it challenging to achieve your muscle-building goals.
2. **Physical Pain:** Injuries can cause pain, discomfort, and, in severe cases, lead to chronic issues that affect your quality of life.
3. **Psychological Impact:** Suffering an injury can be emotionally taxing, leading to frustration, disappointment, and demotivation.

4. **Financial Costs:** Treating injuries, especially severe ones, can incur significant medical expenses and time off work.
5. **Long-Term Consequences:** Neglected or improperly managed injuries may have long-term consequences, affecting your ability to train effectively and maintain a healthy lifestyle.
6. **Lifestyle Disruption:** Injuries can disrupt your daily routine, impacting not only your training but also your work, family life, and social activities.

Common Causes of Injuries in Muscle Building

Understanding the common causes of injuries in muscle building is the first step in prevention. Some of the primary factors contributing to injuries include:

1. **Overtraining:** Pushing your body beyond its limits, training too frequently, or using excessive weights can lead to overuse injuries.
2. **Poor Technique:** Executing exercises with improper form can strain muscles and joints, leading to injuries.
3. **Neglected Warm-Up:** Skipping a proper warm-up can result in muscle strains and other injuries.
4. **Lack of Rest:** Inadequate rest and recovery between workouts can increase the risk of overuse injuries.
5. **Nutritional Deficiencies:** Poor nutrition can lead to muscle imbalances and weakness, making the body more susceptible to injuries.
6. **Inadequate Hydration:** Dehydration can affect muscle function and coordination, increasing the risk of injuries.
7. **Ignoring Pain:** Ignoring pain or discomfort during training can exacerbate minor issues into more severe injuries.
8. **Insufficient Mobility and Flexibility:** Poor joint mobility and limited flexibility can lead to muscle imbalances and injuries.

The Principles of Injury Prevention

Injury prevention is a multifaceted endeavor that requires a combination of strategies, encompassing both proactive and reactive measures. Here are the key principles of injury prevention in muscle building:

1. Proper Warm-Up

A thorough warm-up is essential to prepare your body for the rigors of resistance training. It increases blood flow to your muscles, enhances joint mobility, and readies your nervous system for exercise. A typical warm-up should include light cardiovascular activity, dynamic stretches, and specific warm-up sets for your resistance exercises.

2. Progressive Overload

The principle of progressive overload involves gradually increasing the intensity of your workouts to stimulate muscle growth. However, progression should be gradual and well-planned to prevent overuse injuries. Keep detailed training logs to track your progress and avoid sudden jumps in weight or volume.

3. Technique and Form

Proper technique and form are paramount in preventing injuries. Pay meticulous attention to your exercise execution, focusing on maintaining the correct posture, joint alignment, and movement patterns. If you're unsure about proper form, seek guidance from a qualified trainer.

4. Balance and Symmetry

Muscle imbalances can increase the risk of injuries. Ensure that your training program is well-rounded, targeting all muscle groups equally. Additionally, work on balance and symmetry by incorporating unilateral exercises and corrective movements.

5. Rest and Recovery

Adequate rest and recovery are crucial for injury prevention. Overtraining can lead to overuse injuries and burnout. Include rest days in your training schedule, prioritize sleep, and consider periodic deload weeks to allow your body to recuperate.

6. Nutrition and Hydration

Proper nutrition is essential for muscle building and injury prevention. Ensure you consume a well-balanced diet with sufficient macronutrients, vitamins, and minerals. Hydration is equally important to maintain muscle function and prevent cramps and injuries.

7. Mobility and Flexibility

Improving joint mobility and flexibility can enhance your range of motion, reduce the risk of muscle imbalances, and help you maintain proper form during exercises. Incorporate stretching and mobility exercises into your routine.

8. Injury-Specific Training

If you have a history of injuries or specific vulnerabilities, consider injury-specific training to target weak areas and prevent future problems. A physical therapist or qualified trainer can help design a personalized program.

9. Active Recovery

Active recovery days can be an excellent strategy for preventing injuries. Engage in low-intensity activities like walking, cycling, or swimming on your rest days to promote circulation, alleviate muscle soreness, and maintain joint health.

Common Muscle-Building Injuries and Their Management

Despite your best efforts, injuries can still occur. Understanding common muscle-building injuries and their management is crucial for a swift and effective recovery. Here are some prevalent injuries:

1. Strains and Sprains

Causes: Strains occur when muscle fibers stretch or tear, while sprains affect ligaments. Overstretching or improper form during resistance training can lead to strains and sprains.

Management: Rest, ice, compression, and elevation (RICE) is the initial treatment for mild strains and sprains. Severe cases may require physical therapy or surgery.

2. Tendonitis

Causes: Tendonitis is inflammation of a tendon, often resulting from overuse or repetitive movements. Weightlifting and resistance training can contribute to this condition.

Management: Rest, ice, and anti-inflammatory medications can alleviate the initial pain. Physical therapy and eccentric exercises may be needed for long-term recovery.

3. Rotator Cuff Injuries

Causes: Overhead exercises, such as shoulder presses, can lead to rotator cuff injuries. These injuries often result from poor form or overloading.

Management: Initial treatment may involve rest, ice, and anti-inflammatory medications. Physical therapy and specific exercises are often necessary for recovery.

4. Lower Back Pain

Causes: Poor form during squats, deadlifts, or bent-over rows can lead to lower back pain and injuries.

Management: Rest and anti-inflammatory medications can provide relief. Physical therapy and strengthening exercises may be required for long-term recovery.

5. Patellar Tendonitis (Jumper's Knee)

Causes: Patellar tendonitis is common in athletes who perform repetitive jumping motions, such as squats and leg presses.

Management: Rest, ice, and anti-inflammatory medications can alleviate initial pain. Physical therapy and eccentric exercises are often prescribed.

6. Shin Splints

Causes: Shin splints result from overuse or repetitive impact, often associated with running or jumping.

Management: Rest, ice, and anti-inflammatory medications can help alleviate pain. Proper footwear and orthotics may be recommended to prevent recurrence.

7. Muscle Cramps

Causes: Muscle cramps can occur due to dehydration, electrolyte imbalances, or overuse of a specific muscle group.

Management: Immediate relief can often be achieved through gentle stretching, massage, and hydration. Prevention involves maintaining proper hydration and electrolyte balance.

8. Stress Fractures

Causes: Stress fractures are small cracks in bones that can result from repetitive impact, overuse, or insufficient rest.

Management: Rest is the primary treatment for stress fractures, allowing the bone to heal. Gradual return to exercise is essential to prevent re-injury.

Injury Prevention as Part of Your Training Regimen

Injury prevention should be integrated seamlessly into your training regimen, becoming an inherent aspect of your approach to muscle building. Consider these strategies to make injury prevention a fundamental part of your journey:

1. Regular Self-Assessment

Periodically assess your technique, form, and posture during exercises. Identify any muscle imbalances or joint mobility issues that may be contributing to the risk of injury.

2. Warm-Up and Cool Down

Never skip your warm-up and cool-down routines. They are essential for preparing your body for exercise and aiding in the recovery process.

3. Listen to Your Body

Pay close attention to any signs of discomfort or pain during your workouts. If you experience pain that is more than mild muscle soreness, stop the exercise and seek guidance from a healthcare professional.

4. Seek Professional Guidance

Consider working with a qualified personal trainer, physical therapist, or sports medicine specialist. They can help you design a safe and effective training program, correct your form, and address any imbalances or weaknesses.

5. Gradual Progression

Embrace the principle of gradual progression in your training. Avoid the temptation to lift excessively heavy weights or perform excessive volume without proper preparation.

6. Quality Over Quantity

Focus on the quality of your workouts rather than the quantity. Effective muscle building does not require endless hours in the gym; it demands smart, focused, and efficient training.

7. Recovery Strategies

Incorporate recovery strategies into your routine. This may include massage, foam rolling, stretching, and techniques such as contrast baths to alleviate muscle soreness and improve circulation.

8. Stay Hydrated and Well-Nourished

Proper hydration and nutrition are cornerstones of injury prevention. Maintain balanced electrolytes and consume a well-rounded diet to support muscle function and recovery.

9. Adapt and Modify

Be flexible and willing to modify your training program when needed. If you experience discomfort or pain, adjust your exercises and intensity to accommodate your body's needs.

The Art of Overcoming Setbacks

In the journey of muscle building, setbacks and injuries are not a matter of "if" but "when." When faced with setbacks, it's essential to embrace a positive mindset and a proactive approach to recovery:

1. Seek Professional Guidance

If you sustain an injury, consult a healthcare professional for an accurate diagnosis and treatment plan. Prompt and appropriate care can significantly expedite recovery.

2. Follow Your Rehabilitation Plan

Adhere to your rehabilitation plan diligently. This may include physical therapy exercises, rest, and specific treatments prescribed by your healthcare provider.

3. Patience and Persistence

Understand that the road to recovery may be long and challenging. Be patient, and stay persistent in your efforts to regain your strength and health.

4. Maintain a Positive Mindset

A positive mindset can have a profound impact on recovery. Focus on the progress you make, no matter how small, and use setbacks as opportunities to learn and grow.

5. Reassess and Adjust

Use your setback as an opportunity to reassess your training program, form, and technique. Identify any areas that may have contributed to the injury and make necessary adjustments.

6. Gradual Return

When your healthcare provider gives the green light, gradually ease back into training. Start with lower intensities and volumes, and pay close attention to your body's response.

7. Adapted Training

Consider modified or alternative exercises that are gentler on your body as you recover. Focus on rebuilding your strength and mobility before returning to your previous routine.

Conclusion

In the pursuit of muscle mastery, injury prevention and management are non-negotiable components of success. The path to a chiseled physique is not without its perils, but with a comprehensive understanding of injury prevention principles, a proactive approach to safety, and a willingness to adapt and persevere, you can navigate the obstacles with grace and determination.

Muscle building is not merely a physical journey; it's a testament to your resilience, patience, and unwavering commitment to excellence. Through the art of injury prevention and management, you can safeguard your path, fortify your body, and emerge as a true masterpiece of strength and vitality.

12. TRACKING AND MEASURING PROGRESS

The pursuit of a sculpted, muscular physique is a journey of discipline, dedication, and unwavering commitment. In the art of muscle building, progress is the compass that guides your efforts, measuring your distance from where you began and charting your course to where you aspire to be. But progress, much like the path itself, is not a one-size-fits-all concept. It is multifaceted and can be achieved through various means. In this comprehensive guide, we will explore the intricacies of tracking and measuring progress in the art of muscle building, equipping you with the tools and knowledge to navigate your journey with clarity and purpose.

The Significance of Progress Tracking

Tracking your progress is essential for several reasons:

1. **Motivation:** Observing positive changes in your physique, strength, and performance can be highly motivating. It reinforces your commitment and boosts your morale.
2. **Accountability:** Progress tracking holds you accountable for your actions. When you record your journey, you become more aware of your efforts and their outcomes.
3. **Adjustments:** Tracking allows you to make informed adjustments to your training, nutrition, and recovery strategies. When you identify what works and what doesn't, you can optimize your approach.
4. **Goal Setting:** To reach your destination, you need to know where you're starting and where you want to go. Progress

tracking helps you set realistic and achievable goals.
5. **Preventing Plateaus:** By monitoring your progress, you can detect plateaus or stagnation early and take action to overcome them.
6. **Self-Awareness:** It fosters self-awareness and mindfulness. You become attuned to your body's responses, enabling you to fine-tune your training and nutrition based on how you feel.

Different Dimensions of Progress

Progress in muscle building is multidimensional, encompassing various aspects of your physical and mental development. These dimensions of progress include:

1. Muscle Growth

Muscle hypertrophy is the cornerstone of muscle building. Tracking the size of your muscle groups, such as your chest, biceps, and quads, is a fundamental measure of your progress.

2. Strength Gain

Enhanced strength is a direct result of resistance training. Tracking your one-rep max (1RM) or your ability to lift heavier weights in various exercises demonstrates your strength progress.

3. Endurance Improvement

Endurance is the capacity to sustain physical effort over extended periods. It is particularly important for high-repetition, low-weight resistance training or cardiovascular exercises.

4. Body Composition Changes

Changes in body composition encompass alterations in body fat percentage, muscle mass, and overall body weight. Tracking these factors provides insights into your transformation.

5. Physical Performance

Improvements in your performance during workouts, such as increased reps, decreased rest times, or higher training volumes, indicate progress.

6. Nutritional Adaptation

Your nutrition plays a crucial role in muscle building. Monitoring your dietary intake and adjusting it according to your goals is a measure of nutritional progress.

7. Recovery and Energy Levels

How quickly you recover from workouts and the energy levels you experience daily are significant indicators of progress. Enhanced recovery and sustained energy are key to consistent training and muscle development.

8. Psychological Well-Being

Progress is not solely physical; it's also psychological. Feeling happier, more confident, and less stressed as a result of your fitness journey is a valuable dimension of progress.

Methods of Progress Tracking

Now that we understand the importance of tracking progress and the different dimensions of progress, let's explore various methods and tools that can aid in your tracking efforts:

1. Training Log

A training log is a fundamental tool for tracking your workouts. It should include details such as exercises, sets, reps, weights, rest periods, and perceived effort. Using a training app or journal can help you identify trends and assess your progress.

2. Body Measurements

Taking body measurements, such as chest, waist, hips, and various muscle groups, provides data on your physique changes. You can use a simple tape measure to record these measurements regularly.

3. Progress Photos

Progress photos are visual records of your physique. Taking photos from various angles under consistent lighting conditions is a reliable way to monitor muscle growth and fat loss.

4. Strength Testing

Periodically test your strength with one-rep max (1RM) or submaximal strength tests. This method provides direct feedback on your ability to lift heavier weights.

5. Endurance Challenges

Endurance challenges, such as time trials, high-repetition sets, or long-duration cardio sessions, can be used to assess your cardiovascular endurance progress.

6. Bioelectrical Impedance Scales

Bioelectrical impedance scales are designed to estimate body fat percentage and muscle mass. While not as precise as other methods, they offer a quick and easy way to track body composition.

7. Skinfold Calipers

Skinfold calipers are used to measure skinfold thickness at specific sites on your body. These measurements can be used to estimate body fat percentage.

8. Nutrition Tracking Apps

Nutrition tracking apps allow you to record your dietary intake, including calories, macronutrients, and micronutrients. They can help you align your nutrition with your muscle-building goals.

9. Sleep and Recovery Monitoring

Wearable devices or apps can track your sleep patterns and recovery metrics, providing insights into your overall well-being and the effectiveness of your rest.

10. Performance Metrics

Track your performance metrics during workouts, such as the number of sets completed, rest times, and how quickly you recover between exercises.

Goal Setting and Progress Monitoring

Setting clear, achievable goals is a vital aspect of progress tracking. Your goals should be:

- **Specific:** Clearly define what you want to achieve. Instead of saying, "I want to build muscle," specify, "I want to increase my bench press by 10% in the next three months."
- **Measurable:** Ensure your goals are quantifiable. Use numbers or metrics to track your progress, such as lifting a certain weight, running a particular distance, or reducing body fat percentage.
- **Attainable:** Your goals should be realistic and within reach. While it's essential to challenge yourself, setting unattainable objectives can be demotivating.
- **Relevant:** Your goals should align with your overall objectives and values. They should have meaning and relevance to your life.
- **Time-Bound:** Establish a time frame for achieving your goals. Having a deadline creates a sense of urgency and accountability.

Regularly revisit and adjust your goals as you progress. Consider both short-term and long-term goals to maintain motivation and celebrate smaller victories along the way.

Common Progress Tracking Challenges

Progress tracking is not without its challenges and potential pitfalls:

1. **Inconsistency:** Irregular tracking or data collection can lead to inaccurate assessments of your progress.
2. **Emotional Attachment:** Placing too much emotional attachment to the data can be detrimental to your mental well-being. Remember that progress is not always linear, and setbacks can occur.
3. **Overreliance on the Scale:** Relying solely on the scale can be misleading, as it doesn't account for changes in muscle mass or body composition.

4. **Comparisons to Others:** Comparing your progress to others can lead to frustration and demotivation. Focus on your journey and objectives.
5. **Data Overload:** Collecting an excess of data can be overwhelming. It's essential to identify key metrics that align with your goals and focus on those.
6. **Neglecting the Mind-Body Connection:** Progress isn't just physical; it's also mental. Your mental and emotional well-being plays a vital role in your journey.

Strategies for Effective Progress Tracking

To overcome these challenges and ensure effective progress tracking, consider the following strategies:

1. Establish a Consistent Routine

Set specific times and intervals for tracking your progress. Whether it's daily, weekly, or monthly, consistency is key to accurate assessment.

2. Use Multiple Metrics

Rely on a combination of metrics to gain a comprehensive understanding of your progress. Use body measurements, strength testing, and visual assessments.

3. Celebrate Small Wins

Acknowledge and celebrate even the smallest victories along your journey. Recognizing your progress, no matter how minor, can boost motivation.

4. Focus on the Long-Term

Avoid fixating on short-term fluctuations or plateaus. Keep your long-term goals in mind, and remember that progress may have its ups and downs.

5. Seek Professional Guidance

Consider working with a fitness trainer, nutritionist, or coach who can help you set realistic goals and monitor your progress effectively.

6. Mindfulness and Mind-Body Connection

Pay attention to how your body feels and responds to training, nutrition, and recovery. Mindfulness can provide valuable insights into your progress.

Celebrating Progress Beyond the Numbers

While numbers, measurements, and data are essential for tracking progress in the art of muscle building, it's equally crucial to celebrate progress beyond the quantifiable metrics. Here are some non-numeric achievements to recognize and appreciate:

- **Improved Confidence:** As your physical appearance and abilities change, your confidence and self-esteem often see significant improvements.
- **Enhanced Discipline:** Committing to a training and nutrition plan requires discipline. The development of this discipline is a notable accomplishment in itself.
- **Resilience:** The ability to overcome setbacks and plateaus demonstrates resilience and mental fortitude.
- **Lifestyle Changes:** Positive changes in your lifestyle, such as better sleep, improved dietary choices, and reduced stress, contribute to your overall well-being.
- **Enjoyment:** Finding joy in your workouts, nutrition, and the overall process of muscle building is an achievement worth celebrating.
- **Inspiration to Others:** Your progress can inspire and motivate others on their fitness journeys.

The Art of Reflection and Adaptation

Progress tracking is a dynamic process that involves reflection and adaptation. Regularly reviewing your data, analyzing trends, and adjusting your approach are crucial components of this process. Ask yourself the following questions:

- **What is working well in my current routine?**
- **What aspects of my training, nutrition, or recovery need improvement?**

- **Am I on track to achieve my short-term and long-term goals?**
- **What obstacles or challenges have I encountered, and how can I overcome them?**
- **Do I need to adjust my goals based on my progress and current circumstances?**

Adaptation is a key element in the art of muscle building. Be open to making changes, whether they involve your training program, nutritional choices, or recovery strategies. Remember that your journey is unique, and your approach should be tailored to your individual needs and objectives.

Conclusion

Progress tracking in the art of muscle building is a multifaceted endeavor that combines numbers, metrics, and personal growth. It is a compass that guides your journey, helping you navigate the complexities of training, nutrition, and recovery. As you continue to sculpt your physique and enhance your physical capabilities, remember that progress is more than just numbers on a page; it is a testament to your dedication and a reflection of your unwavering commitment to self-improvement.

In the art of muscle building, progress tracking is not a mere tool; it is an art form in itself, requiring mindfulness, patience, and adaptability. Embrace the journey, celebrate your achievements, and use the data as a guide on your path to becoming a masterpiece of strength and vitality.

13. MOTIVATION AND MENTAL TOUGHNESS

The pursuit of muscle mastery is a journey that transcends the physical realm. It's a testament to the power of determination, resilience, and unwavering commitment. While the art of muscle building involves lifting weights, sculpting physiques, and achieving physical prowess, it's the unseen forces of motivation and mental toughness that truly fuel the engine of success. In this comprehensive guide, we will explore the intricacies of motivation and mental toughness in the context of muscle building, equipping you with the knowledge and strategies to harness these forces and elevate your journey to new heights.

The Role of Motivation

Motivation is the inner fire that propels us to take action, make choices, and strive for goals. In the realm of muscle building, motivation is the driving force that sustains our commitment to training, nutrition, and recovery. Without motivation, the path can become arduous and the journey daunting. Let's delve into the significance of motivation and how to cultivate it effectively.

1. Intrinsic vs. Extrinsic Motivation

Motivation can be categorized into two primary types: intrinsic and extrinsic.

- **Intrinsic motivation** comes from within. It's the desire to engage in an activity because it's personally rewarding. For muscle building, intrinsic motivation might stem from a

genuine love for lifting weights, the joy of setting and achieving fitness goals, or the satisfaction of feeling strong and capable.
- **Extrinsic motivation** originates from external sources, such as rewards, recognition, or avoidance of punishment. It's the motivation to engage in an activity for the sake of an external outcome, like winning a bodybuilding competition or impressing others with your physique.

While both forms of motivation have their place, intrinsic motivation tends to be more enduring and effective in the context of muscle building. Cultivating a genuine love for the journey and a deep connection to the process can sustain your motivation over the long term.

2. Identifying Your Why

Understanding your "why" is a powerful motivator. Your "why" is the deep-seated reason behind your muscle-building journey. It's the driving force that keeps you committed even when faced with challenges and setbacks. Your "why" might include reasons like improving your health, boosting self-esteem, or setting an example for your loved ones.

Take time to reflect on your "why" and write it down. This written declaration can serve as a constant reminder of your motivations and keep you on track when enthusiasm wanes.

3. Setting SMART Goals

Setting clear, specific, and achievable goals is a fundamental aspect of motivation. SMART goals are:

- **Specific:** Clearly defined and unambiguous.
- **Measurable:** Quantifiable to track progress.
- **Achievable:** Realistic and attainable within your capabilities.
- **Relevant:** Aligned with your "why" and meaningful to you.
- **Time-bound:** Defined within a specific timeframe or deadline.

For example, a SMART goal could be: "I will increase my bench press by 10% within the next three months to improve my upper body strength and overall physique."

4. Visualizing Success

Visualization is a powerful technique to enhance motivation. Envision yourself reaching your fitness goals, whether it's sporting a chiseled physique, setting a new personal record, or completing a challenging workout. This mental rehearsal can boost your confidence, reinforce your commitment, and make your goals feel more achievable.

5. Finding Inspiration

Surrounding yourself with inspirational figures, whether they're renowned bodybuilders, fitness influencers, or peers on similar journeys, can provide a motivational boost. The stories and successes of others can serve as beacons of inspiration and remind you of what's possible.

The Importance of Mental Toughness

Mental toughness is the ability to persist and perform optimally despite adversity, discomfort, or challenges. In the context of muscle building, it is the unwavering mental fortitude that enables you to push through grueling workouts, adhere to your nutrition plan, and overcome setbacks. Let's explore the significance of mental toughness and how to cultivate this invaluable trait.

1. Embracing Discomfort

Discomfort is an inherent part of muscle building. The physical strain, muscle soreness, and fatigue are all facets of the journey. Embracing discomfort as a natural and necessary part of the process can strengthen your mental toughness. Rather than avoiding or dreading it, learn to welcome discomfort as a sign of growth.

2. Setting a Growth Mindset

A growth mindset is the belief that abilities and intelligence can be developed through dedication and hard work. Cultivating a growth mindset can enhance your mental toughness by framing challenges as opportunities for improvement rather than insurmountable obstacles.

3. Overcoming Plateaus

Plateaus are a common occurrence in muscle building. They can be frustrating and demotivating, but they are also opportunities to develop mental toughness. Instead of succumbing to plateaus, use them as a catalyst to push through and refine your approach.

4. Resilience in the Face of Setbacks

Setbacks, whether they're injuries, missed workouts, or lapses in nutrition, are inevitable. Mental toughness empowers you to bounce back from setbacks and adapt your strategy. It's the resilience to view setbacks as temporary detours rather than roadblocks.

5. Developing Focus and Discipline

Mental toughness is closely linked to focus and discipline. It's the ability to stay on course and resist distractions, temptations, and negative self-talk. Developing a strong sense of discipline and focus can fortify your mental toughness.

Strategies to Cultivate Mental Toughness

Cultivating mental toughness is an ongoing process that requires dedication and practice. Here are strategies to develop and strengthen this vital trait:

1. Progressive Exposure to Challenges

Gradually expose yourself to increasingly challenging situations. This could involve incrementally heavier weights, more demanding workouts, or more complex exercises. The consistent exposure to challenges can bolster your mental toughness.

2. Mindfulness and Meditation

Practicing mindfulness and meditation can enhance your mental resilience. These techniques teach you to remain present, manage stress, and improve your capacity to deal with adversity.

3. Self-Talk and Positive Affirmations

The way you talk to yourself can significantly impact your mental toughness. Replace negative self-talk with positive affirmations. Encourage and uplift yourself during challenging moments.

4. Learn from Adversity

Instead of viewing adversity as setbacks, approach them as learning experiences. Analyze what went wrong and how you can improve. Every adversity can be a stepping stone to mental growth.

5. Set and Conquer Small Challenges

Setting and conquering small, achievable challenges can build your confidence and mental toughness. These victories can serve as building blocks for tackling larger challenges.

6. Find a Support System

Seek support from friends, training partners, or coaches who understand your journey. Sharing your experiences and challenges with a supportive network can enhance your resilience.

The Synergy of Motivation and Mental Toughness

While motivation and mental toughness are distinct concepts, they are interconnected and complement each other in the art of muscle building.

- **Motivation ignites the spark:** It fuels your desire to embark on the journey, set goals, and take action. Motivation is the initial catalyst that propels you forward.
- **Mental toughness keeps the flame burning:** Once the initial motivation wanes, mental toughness steps in to sustain your efforts. It ensures you persist even when the journey becomes challenging or monotonous.
- **Motivation rekindles the fire:** As you overcome obstacles and witness progress, your motivation can be reignited. Each accomplishment becomes a source of inspiration, breathing new life into your journey.

Together, these forces create a dynamic cycle of progression. Motivation initiates the journey, mental toughness sustains it, and the fruits of your labor rekindle your motivation, perpetuating the cycle.

Overcoming Challenges to Motivation and Mental Toughness

Challenges to motivation and mental toughness are common and often unavoidable. Understanding these challenges and implementing strategies to overcome them is essential for maintaining consistency and resilience.

1. Burnout and Overtraining

Excessive training without adequate rest and recovery can lead to burnout and a decline in motivation. To overcome this challenge, ensure you incorporate rest days in your training regimen, adjust training intensity periodically, and listen to your body's signals for rest.

2. Plateaus and Stagnation

Reaching plateaus can be demotivating and test your mental toughness. To combat stagnation, consider adjusting your training routine, introducing new exercises, and modifying your nutrition plan.

3. Negative Self-Talk and Self-Doubt

Negative self-talk can erode your motivation and mental toughness. Combat self-doubt with positive affirmations, visualization, and a strong support network.

4. Lack of Progress

Lack of noticeable progress can lead to frustration and demotivation. To overcome this, focus on small wins, celebrate your achievements, and remind yourself of your "why."

5. Life Stressors

External stressors, such as work, family, or personal issues, can impact motivation and mental toughness. It's crucial to manage stress effectively through techniques like mindfulness, meditation, and time management.

Conclusion

In the art of muscle building, motivation and mental toughness are the unsung heroes that propel you toward mastery. They are the driving forces that power your journey, keep you committed, and empower you to overcome obstacles. While the physical aspects of muscle building are essential, it's the unseen forces of the mind that truly shape your path to success.

Embrace motivation as the spark that ignites your journey, and nurture mental toughness as the unyielding force that sustains it. As you cultivate these forces and navigate the complexities of muscle building, remember that your journey is a testament to your inner strength and resilience. In the pursuit of muscle mastery, motivation and mental toughness are the unseen forces that transform a desire into a reality and a dream into a masterpiece of strength and vitality.

14. FINE-TUNING YOUR ROUTINE FOR RESULTS

In the realm of muscle building, the concept of a "routine" is the cornerstone of success. Your routine encompasses your training program, nutrition plan, recovery strategies, and lifestyle choices. The art of muscle building is not a one-size-fits-all endeavor; it's a dynamic and personalized journey that requires continuous refinement and optimization. In this comprehensive guide, we will explore the intricacies of fine-tuning your routine for optimal results, equipping you with the knowledge and strategies to elevate your muscle-building journey to new heights.

The Foundation: A Well-Structured Training Program

Your training program is the beating heart of your muscle-building routine. It is the structured plan that guides your workouts, dictates your exercises, sets your intensity, and determines your progression. A well-structured training program is the keystone of your routine and the source of physical transformation. Let's delve into the key components of an effective training program:

1. Periodization

Periodization is the strategic planning of your training program over time. It involves dividing your training into distinct phases, each with specific objectives. Common phases include hypertrophy (muscle building), strength, and power. Periodization prevents plateaus, optimizes results, and minimizes the risk of overtraining.

2. Exercise Selection

Selecting the right exercises is crucial. Compound exercises like squats, deadlifts, bench presses, and pull-ups are foundational for muscle building as they engage multiple muscle groups simultaneously. Accessory exercises target specific muscles and help address imbalances.

3. Volume and Intensity

Volume refers to the total amount of work in your workouts, which is a product of sets, reps, and weight. Intensity relates to how close you're training to your one-rep max (1RM). Balancing volume and intensity is key to muscle building. Higher volume (more sets and reps) with moderate intensity is often used for hypertrophy.

4. Progressive Overload

Progressive overload is the practice of gradually increasing the demands on your muscles to stimulate growth. It can be achieved by adding weight, increasing reps, or shortening rest periods over time. Without progressive overload, your muscles won't have a reason to grow.

5. Frequency and Split

Training frequency refers to how often you work each muscle group. A muscle group can be trained 2-3 times per week for optimal hypertrophy. Split routines divide muscle groups into separate training sessions, allowing for focused work and adequate recovery.

6. Rest and Recovery

Adequate rest and recovery are essential. Muscles grow during rest, not during workouts. Ensure you get enough sleep, prioritize rest days, and incorporate active recovery techniques like stretching and mobility work.

7. Form and Technique

Proper form and technique are non-negotiable. Executing exercises with correct form minimizes the risk of injury and maximizes muscle engagement. If you're unsure of your form, consider working with a qualified trainer or coach.

8. Tracking and Measuring Progress

Regularly track your progress to ensure you're making gains and identify areas that need improvement. Utilize tools like training logs, body measurements, and performance metrics to measure your journey's success.

The Fuel: Optimizing Nutrition for Muscle Growth

Nutrition is the fuel that powers your muscle-building engine. Your dietary choices have a profound impact on your ability to gain muscle, recover from workouts, and achieve your physique goals. Fine-tuning your nutrition plan is an essential aspect of your muscle-building routine. Let's explore the key components of an effective muscle-building diet:

1. Caloric Surplus

To build muscle, you must consume more calories than you burn. This creates a caloric surplus, providing the energy and nutrients your body needs for muscle growth. However, the surplus should be controlled to minimize fat gain.

2. Protein Intake

Protein is the building block of muscle. It's essential for muscle repair and growth. Aim for a protein intake of around 1.6 to 2.2 grams per kilogram of body weight. Quality sources of protein include lean meats, fish, poultry, dairy, and plant-based options like beans and tofu.

3. Carbohydrates and Fats

Carbohydrates provide the energy required for intense workouts, while fats are essential for overall health. Balance your carbohydrate and fat intake based on your energy needs and personal preferences. Whole grains, fruits, vegetables, and healthy fats like avocados and nuts should be staples in your diet.

4. Meal Timing and Frequency

Eating at the right times is crucial. Pre-workout meals provide energy for exercise, while post-workout meals support recovery. Meal frequency can vary, but consuming protein at regular intervals throughout the day is advisable.

5. Hydration

Staying adequately hydrated is often overlooked but is critical for muscle function, recovery, and overall health. Ensure you consume enough water throughout the day, and consider the use of electrolyte-rich beverages during intense workouts.

6. Supplementation

Supplements can be used to fill nutritional gaps, but they should not replace whole foods. Common muscle-building supplements include whey protein, creatine, branched-chain amino acids (BCAAs), and multivitamins. Consult with a healthcare professional before starting any supplement regimen.

7. Adaptation to Progress

As your training and goals evolve, so should your nutrition plan. Adjust your caloric intake and macronutrient ratios to align with your changing needs and objectives.

The Recovery: Prioritizing Rest and Regeneration

Recovery is an often underestimated aspect of muscle building. Your body needs time to repair and grow, and fine-tuning your recovery strategies can significantly impact your results. Let's explore the key components of effective recovery:

1. Sleep

Adequate sleep is the foundation of recovery. During deep sleep, your body releases growth hormone and repairs damaged tissues. Aim for 7-9 hours of quality sleep per night.

2. Active Recovery

Active recovery techniques like stretching, foam rolling, and mobility work can enhance circulation, reduce muscle soreness, and improve flexibility. Incorporate these practices into your routine, especially on rest days.

3. Nutrition

Nutrition plays a vital role in recovery. After intense workouts, consume a meal or snack that includes both carbohydrates and protein to kickstart the recovery process.

4. Hydration

Dehydration can impair muscle function and slow down recovery. Ensure you stay well-hydrated throughout the day and especially during workouts.

5. Stress Management

High stress levels can hinder recovery. Implement stress management techniques like meditation, deep breathing, and mindfulness to support your body's healing processes.

6. Periodic Deloading

Periodic deloading is a planned reduction in training intensity and volume. Deloading weeks give your body a chance to recover and prevent overtraining.

7. Listen to Your Body

Your body provides valuable feedback. Pay attention to signs of overtraining, fatigue, or chronic soreness. When your body signals the need for rest, heed its call.

The Lifestyle: Building Healthy Habits

Your lifestyle choices have a significant impact on your muscle-building routine. Building healthy habits that support your goals is essential. Let's explore lifestyle factors that can fine-tune your muscle-building journey:

1. Consistency

Consistency is the linchpin of muscle building. Stick to your training and nutrition plan over the long term. Results are achieved through cumulative effort and dedication.

2. Mindset and Motivation

Cultivate a positive mindset and motivation. Remember your "why" and the reasons you embarked on this journey. Surround yourself with motivational cues and a support system that uplifts you.

3. Limiting Stressors

High stress levels can negatively impact muscle-building progress. Identify stressors in your life and take steps to reduce or manage them effectively.

4. Rest and Leisure

Include leisure and rest in your routine. A well-rounded life with relaxation, hobbies, and social activities enhances your overall well-being and supports your muscle-building efforts.

5. Goal Setting and Tracking

Set clear, achievable goals and track your progress. Regularly revisiting your goals and adjusting your routine keeps you aligned with your objectives.

6. Seeking Professional Guidance

Consider working with a qualified fitness trainer, nutritionist, or coach who can provide personalized guidance and ensure you're on the right path.

7. Staying Informed

The field of fitness and nutrition is continually evolving. Stay informed about the latest research, training techniques, and nutrition strategies to optimize your routine.

Common Challenges and Pitfalls

Fine-tuning your routine also involves addressing common challenges and pitfalls that can hinder your progress. Awareness of these obstacles and strategies to overcome them is essential:

1. Plateaus

Reaching plateaus is normal. To overcome them, adjust your training program, nutrition plan, or recovery strategies. Plateaus are opportunities for growth and refinement.

2. Inconsistent Progress

Not all progress will be linear. Some weeks may yield exceptional results, while others may seem stagnant. Focus on the long-term trend of improvement and remain patient.

3. Nutrition Challenges

Nutrition can be a major challenge. Social events, travel, and cravings can disrupt your dietary routine. Plan ahead, practice moderation, and find strategies to maintain dietary discipline.

4. Time Constraints

Many individuals have busy schedules. Finding time for workouts, meal preparation, and rest can be a challenge. Prioritize your health and make time for the habits that support your muscle-building journey.

5. Comparisons and Self-Doubt

Comparing your progress to others or doubting your capabilities can be demotivating. Remember that everyone's journey is unique. Focus on your own path and the progress you're making.

Conclusion

Fine-tuning your routine for optimal muscle-building results is a continuous process that involves the science of training and nutrition and the art of adaptation. Your journey is a dynamic and personalized experience that requires diligence, patience, and a commitment to growth.

As you navigate the complexities of muscle building, remember that the routine you create is a reflection of your goals, your dedication, and your aspirations. It is a living, evolving entity that adapts to your changing needs and objectives. By honing your training program, optimizing your nutrition, prioritizing recovery, and embracing a healthy lifestyle, you empower yourself to sculpt your body and elevate your physical capabilities. In the art of muscle building, your routine is the brush with which you paint the masterpiece of strength and vitality.

15. CASE STUDIES AND SUCCESS STORIES

In the pursuit of muscle mastery, one of the most invaluable resources at your disposal is the knowledge and experience of those who have walked the path before you. Case studies and success stories are like treasure troves of insights, providing a glimpse into the journeys of individuals who have achieved remarkable transformations and reached their muscle-building goals. In this comprehensive guide, we will explore real-life case studies and success stories, offering you a deeper understanding of the art of muscle building and equipping you with the inspiration, strategies, and blueprints to reach your own pinnacle of success.

The Power of Real-Life Success

Success stories and case studies serve as powerful motivators and educational tools. They offer the following benefits:

1. Inspiration: Success stories can inspire you by showing what's possible. Witnessing the achievements of others can ignite your motivation and remind you that your goals are within reach.

2. Practical Insight: Real-life case studies provide practical insights into the strategies, tactics, and routines that have worked for others. Learning from their experiences can help you refine your approach.

3. Motivation for the Journey: The journey of muscle building is long and filled with challenges. Success stories can help you maintain your motivation, especially during challenging times or plateaus.

4. Proof of Concept: Success stories serve as proof that the principles of muscle building actually work. They validate the science and strategies discussed in books, articles, and fitness guides.

The Science and Art of Muscle Building

Before delving into specific case studies and success stories, it's essential to understand the science and art of muscle building. While the principles of muscle building are grounded in science, the individual's journey is a highly personalized and artistic endeavor. Here are the key components that form the foundation of muscle building:

1. Progressive Overload: To build muscle, you must consistently challenge your muscles by progressively increasing the resistance or intensity of your workouts. This is the cornerstone of muscle growth.

2. Nutrition: Adequate nutrition, with a focus on protein intake, caloric surplus, and balanced macronutrients, provides the necessary fuel for muscle growth and recovery.

3. Recovery: Muscles grow during periods of rest and recovery. Adequate sleep, nutrition, and active recovery strategies are essential for optimal results.

4. Training Program: A well-structured training program includes exercise selection, volume, intensity, periodization, and rest periods. It guides your workouts and ensures effective muscle stimulation.

5. Mindset and Motivation: The mental aspect of muscle building is just as important as the physical. Motivation, discipline, and mental toughness are critical for long-term success.

6. Lifestyle Choices: Lifestyle factors such as stress management, consistency, goal setting, and support systems all contribute to a successful muscle-building journey.

Real-Life Transformations: Case Studies

Let's dive into real-life case studies that highlight the transformative power of the principles of muscle building.

Case Study 1: The Weight Loss to Muscle Gain Transformation

Background: John, a 35-year-old professional, had struggled with weight issues for most of his life. He decided to embark on a transformation journey to shed excess fat and build muscle.

Approach:

- John started with a caloric deficit and a focus on cardio workouts to shed excess fat.
- After achieving his desired weight loss, he gradually transitioned into a caloric surplus to support muscle growth.
- He followed a well-structured strength training program that included compound exercises and progressive overload.
- John prioritized protein intake to support muscle recovery and growth.

Results:

- Over the course of 18 months, John transformed his physique. He shed 30 pounds of fat and gained 10 pounds of lean muscle.
- His body fat percentage dropped from 25% to 12%, and he achieved a lean and muscular physique.
- John's experience emphasizes the importance of transitioning between fat loss and muscle gain phases to achieve a balanced transformation.

Case Study 2: The Skinny to Strong Transformation

Background: Emily, a 24-year-old college student, had always been slender and wanted to build strength and muscle for both fitness and confidence.

Approach:

- Emily followed a well-structured strength training program focused on compound exercises and progressive overload.
- She maintained a slight caloric surplus to support muscle growth.

- Protein intake was a priority, with an emphasis on whole foods like lean meats and plant-based sources.
- Emily incorporated active recovery techniques, including yoga and mobility work, to prevent injuries.

Results:

- Over the course of 12 months, Emily gained 15 pounds of lean muscle and significantly improved her strength.
- Her physique transformed from slender to strong and toned.
- Emily's journey illustrates that even individuals with a naturally slim build can achieve substantial muscle growth with the right training and nutrition.

Success Stories: Inspiring Journeys

Success stories are not limited to specific case studies; they encompass a wide range of individuals who have achieved remarkable transformations through dedication, hard work, and the right strategies. Let's explore a few of these inspiring journeys.

Success Story 1: The Overcoming Injury Tale

Background: Alex, a 28-year-old athlete, faced a setback when he suffered a severe knee injury during a sports event. He went through surgery and a lengthy rehabilitation process.

Approach:

- Alex worked closely with a physical therapist to regain strength and mobility in his injured knee.
- He adopted a cautious approach to training, focusing on exercises that did not strain the injured area.
- Nutrition played a pivotal role in his recovery, with an emphasis on anti-inflammatory foods and protein for tissue repair.

Results:

- Over a period of two years, Alex not only regained his pre-injury strength but also surpassed it.

- He returned to his sport with newfound resilience and a more robust physique.
- Alex's journey demonstrates that with patience, determination, and smart strategies, recovery from injuries can lead to a stronger and more resilient body.

Success Story 2: The Lifelong Transformation

Background: Susan, a 50-year-old mother of two, decided to prioritize her health and fitness after years of neglect. She wanted to prove that age is not a barrier to transformation.

Approach:

- Susan adopted a balanced and sustainable nutrition plan, focusing on whole foods and portion control.
- She engaged in regular strength training and cardio workouts, gradually increasing intensity and volume.
- Stress management techniques, including meditation and mindfulness, played a crucial role in her journey.

Results:

- Over the course of five years, Susan transformed her physique and her health.
- She shed 50 pounds of excess weight, built lean muscle, and achieved a toned and vibrant appearance.
- Susan's journey is a testament to the fact that it's never too late to embark on a transformative fitness journey.

Key Lessons and Takeaways

The case studies and success stories shared here offer a wealth of insights and inspiration. Let's distill the key lessons and takeaways that can guide your own muscle-building journey:

1. Set Clear Goals: Define your goals and objectives, whether they involve weight loss, muscle gain, strength improvement, or a holistic transformation of your health and physique.

2. Adapt and Evolve: Be open to adjusting your approach as needed. Periodize your training and nutrition to match your changing goals.

3. Prioritize Recovery: Recovery is just as critical as training. Adequate sleep, nutrition, and rest are the building blocks of muscle growth.

4. Nutrition is Paramount: Pay close attention to your nutrition. Ensure you're consuming enough protein and calories to support your muscle-building goals.

5. Mindset Matters: Cultivate a positive and determined mindset. Mental resilience and motivation are essential for long-term success.

6. Consistency is Key: Consistency in training, nutrition, and lifestyle choices is the bedrock of success. Small, daily efforts compound into significant transformations.

7. Support and Accountability: Seek support from a trainer, coach, or a fitness community to keep you accountable and motivated on your journey.

8. Celebrate Milestones: Recognize and celebrate your achievements, no matter how small. It's these victories that fuel your motivation and determination.

Your Journey, Your Success

As you embark on your own journey of muscle building, remember that every transformation is unique. Your goals, circumstances, and starting point are specific to you. The case studies and success stories presented here serve as blueprints and inspiration, but your path will be your own.

The art of muscle building is a deeply personal and transformative endeavour. It's a testament to your commitment, resilience, and the mastery of both the science and the art of fitness. As you navigate the complexities of this journey, draw inspiration from those who have succeeded before you, adapt their strategies to your unique circumstances, and sculpt your own masterpiece of strength, health, and vitality. Your story, your case study, and your success are waiting to be written.

Milton Keynes UK
Ingram Content Group UK Ltd.
UKHW050639221123
432980UK00014B/735